POWER, LAW, RIGHT, AND LOVE

# POWER, LAW, RIGHT, AND LOVE | *A Study in Political Values*

Edgar H. Brookes

PUBLISHED FOR THE LILLY ENDOWMENT RESEARCH
PROGRAM IN CHRISTIANITY AND POLITICS BY THE
DUKE UNIVERSITY PRESS, DURHAM, N. C.      1963

© 1963, Duke University Press

*Library of Congress Catalog Card 63-18576*

Cambridge University Press, London, N.W. 1, England

The quotation from Rupert Brooke's
"The Dead" on page 40 is reprinted
by permission of Dodd, Mead & Company from *The Collected Poems of
Rupert Brooke* (copyright 1915 by
Dodd, Mead & Company, Inc.; copyright 1943 by Edward Marsh). Permission has also been granted for this
quotation by the holders of the British
copyright, Sidgwick and Jackson, Ltd.,
and of the Canadian copyright, Mc-
Clelland & Stewart.

*Printed in the United States of America
by Heritage Printers, Inc., Charlotte, N. C.*

*Foreword*

The word "love" has become so debased by sentimental usage that we are apt to shy away from it in serious discussion and as a consequence some may be surprised to find love described in the lectures which follow as a political virtue. We accept the word "justice" much more readily as descriptive of the goal of the political process. Yet it is doubtful if justice can be realized if the acts of justice are not inspired by love. It is not a mawkish, sentimental kind of love which the lecturer here celebrates, but a love which includes the claims of justice and goes beyond them. When truly practiced it often involves suffering and always demands self-sacrifices.

But does it pay? Does a just life pay? That question was put to Socrates by the Sophists, and Plato endeavors to answer it in numerous dialogues but particularly in the *Gorgias*. The questions cannot be answered except in the terms in which we view ultimate reality, for, as Plato said, what we love as the good will ultimately determine what we regard as the real. Is death itself the greatest calamity that can befall man? If it is, then not only is love irrelevant to life but so are justice, honor, courage, and all the virtues that distinguish human life from animal existence. Only man is capable of a life of love, a capacity he shares with his Creator. He can and often does fall short of realizing that capacity, but it is the only resource available for transforming a "partnership in law" into a genuine community.

Our lecturer writes as one who has had many years of practical political experience. Born in England in 1897, Dr. Edgar Brookes has spent most of his life in South Africa. From 1933 to 1945 he was Principal of Adams College and most recently has been Professor of History and Political Science at the University of Natal. He has twice served as President of the South African Institute of Race Relations. From 1937 to 1952 he served in the Senate of the South African government as a representative of the natives of Natal and Zululand. From 1945 to 1950 he was a member of the Permanent Native Affairs Commission. His publications include a *History of Native Policy in South Africa* (1923), *Native Education in South Africa* (1929), *South Africa in a Changing World* (1953), *The Native Reserves of Natal* (1956), and *The City of God and the Politics of Crisis* (1960). He was invited to serve as a Visiting Professor of Political Science at Duke University during the spring semester of 1963 and during the course of that semester delivered the three lectures which are published here. His warm and gracious personality have won him the affection and respect of those who have come to know him during his visit to Duke University.

It should be understood that although the publication of this book was made possible by funds provided by Lilly Endowment, Inc., the Endowment is not the author or publisher and is not to be understood as necessarily approving, by virtue of its grant, any of the views expressed in the pages which follow.

John H. Hallowell, *Director*

*Lilly Endowment Research Program*
*in Christianity and Politics*

# Preface

Like every other Lilly lecturer I must thank the Lilly Endowment Research Program in Christianity and Politics for giving me the opportunity of delivering the lectures published in this little book, and with it the privilege of personal contact with Duke University, with the human and academic inspiration which such an experience brings. I am under special obligation to Professor John H. Hallowell for many acts of understanding friendship and help that I shall not soon forget.

That these lectures do not make a very large book I realize, not without some regret; but their brevity need not be a disadvantage, since it may encourage busy men to follow their argument. In their insistence on the vital interrelationship between political action and religious faith they sound a note which is very important in our own day. In emphasizing that love is a political virtue, they are not idealistic but intensely practical. The whole majestic structure of the British Commonwealth has rocked as in an earthquake because justice was not always accompanied by love. The unparalleled and most moving effort of the United States to help the war-weary and underdeveloped countries of the world might end in failure without love. The presence of love would revolutionize the situation in my own country, the Republic of South Africa, in the bleak atmosphere of which nothing else seems able to avoid disaster.

Edgar H. Brookes

*Duke University,*
*Durham, North Carolina*
*February 24, 1963*

# Table of Contents

POWER, LAW, RIGHT, AND LOVE

*Chapter One*

# POWER, LAW, AND RIGHT

In this study we wish to examine some of the fundamentals of human association as seen in the light of our faith. We shall begin with the concept of power — a concept morally neutral but not morally reprehensible. Power may indeed become a positive force for good if it is rightly controlled. The long-accepted belief of mankind is that power should be controlled by law. But the term "law" is ambiguous. In Great Britain it has been defined as "the command of a sovereign Parliament enforced by a sanction." Countries such as the Republic of South Africa and Ghana have constitutions which are closely modeled on that of Great Britain, without the conventions and the spirit which makes British parliamentary sovereignty tolerable. It is therefore necessary, especially with our minds on Africa, to distinguish between "law" and the majestic conception of "right."

But even "right" is not the last word in political philosophy. Though its praises may be sounded by the tongues of men and even of angels, yet without charity it is nothing. At best it can give us the beauty and also the cold aridity of a lunar landscape. The warm, life-giving sun of love is needed to give justice even that light which it undoubtedly shows to the wayfaring man.

The claim that love is a political and not merely a personal virtue is a daring and in some measure an original one. Yet it is in the air, and during the last decade writers such as the Protestant Tillich and the Catholic Riquet have introduced us to it. Its implications in the changing continent of Africa need to be considered by missionaries, administrators, and statesmen.

The general political doctrine here put forward is considered with special reference to Africa, and more particularly to the troubled Republic of South Africa. This making concrete of the theoretical issues will, it is hoped, give strength and reality to the arguments.

Power is of the very essence of the State. The State is the appointed organ — there is no reason to think that it is not the divinely appointed organ — for co-operation. The combination of human beings in action produces power.

It is sometimes thought that the use of force by the State is the result of the fall of man — or, if such a phrase be resented as being too theological, of the need to deal with the criminal fringe of society and the negligence and lack of public spirit of the ordinary citizen. But even in a State of saints force would be needed. Take the building of a road, for example. On this road travel the anarchist, the pacifist, the critic of government. They could not go to a meeting to denounce force if there were no road to travel on. The road cannot be built by the roadside dwellers, for then a hundred yards of good tarred road might be followed by a hundred yards of pot-holes or by a quagmire. The organization of the State is required to build the road, and with that admission we must let in taxation, a budget, a civil service, a legislature and all the apparatus of government. The saints would all agree that there should be a uniform rule of the road, but neither natural justice nor divine revelation tells us whether traffic should travel on the right or on the left, nor what the speed limit should be, and on all these points a decision must be taken and uniformity in adhering to it be enforced.

Jacques Maritain has reminded us that the State is only one organ of the body politic. Do not the other organs also have power to enforce their will? A Church may excommunicate one of its members, and if he believes in its power to do so this may cause him great anguish of spirit, and virtually force him to do what the Church feels is right. In every profession there are forms of ostracism, straightforward or subtle. Let us take the example of Lieutenant Carey, who in 1879, in a moment of panic, galloped off and left the Prince Imperial of France alone to face a horde of Zulu warriors. Carey was acquitted by a court-martial, but when he was sent out to military duty in India no one would speak to him. If he started a conversation he was not answered. If he joined a group it broke up. Such a punishment would do more to break a man's spirit than imprisonment. Still, it is not imprisonment, and it is the monopoly of the State to interfere with a man's liberty, his life, or his property. In this sense the State is unique in its power. No other human society has the same sweeping physical might.

Is power evil? Surely not in itself. Yet power, although neutral in the moral conflict, can be dangerous indeed. A tremendous force of water issuing from a cleft in the rocks of the Alps can be tamed and harnessed to a hydroelectric scheme. Apart from that it may be a spectacle to be enjoyed and also a peril to be avoided. An African river, normally a trickle in a dusty river-bed, may come down after heavy rains as a roaring torrent, spreading death and destruction around it. There is not time to harness it: it can only be avoided and woe to those who cannot avoid it! The only hope (and that in most cases prohibited in large and sparsely populated Africa by expense) would be to control the rare and unpredictable flood by canalization or by building dams. Power, in short, though not in its nature evil, must be put under some kind of restraint if it is to be safe.

Let us examine the statement further and in particular the point that power is not inherently evil. Even the New Testament accepts the power of the State unequivocally. "He beareth not the sword in vain."[1] When the Creed says, "He suffered under Pontius Pilate," it accepts the fact that Pilate's

1. Rom. 13:4.

power was legitimate, however meanly and shamefully he allowed it to be misused. Did not the Divine Sufferer Himself say, "Thou couldest have no power at all against me except it were given thee from above"?[2] Even St. Augustine accepts the power of the Roman Empire and its capacity for being put to good use.[3]

We must therefore condemn clearly, with all due reluctance to criticize views held by men of noble ideals, any tendency to condemn power as such as being neither ethical nor Christian. Although the totalitarian State must be condemned, although injustice, racial discrimination, and genocide must be resisted, the power of the State is in itself neutral, not evil, and may as surely be harnessed for good uses as for bad. Pacifism may possibly be justified by the exceeding horrors of modern warfare or by arguing that no advantages can be obtained from war which will not be more than counterbalanced by losses — though this latter argument cannot be taken for granted in all cases — but it cannot be justified by the proposition that force is somehow inherently wrong. This absolute, like all absolutes except love, leads one, if applied logically, to conclusions that make human life impossible. The same principles which oppose the atom bomb must in all fairness oppose the policeman's baton, the strong right arm that knocks out a drowning man in order to make his rescue possible, and even the mother's correcting hand. In all these cases the abuse does not take away the use. The flogging schoolmaster is not an attractive figure, but must a school have no discipline? To substitute "lines," or in extreme cases expulsion, for flogging is not to expel force: it is only to use another kind of force. To expel a boy is a striking act of force. All that is gained by substituting measures such as these for flogging is to protect the aesthetic susceptibilities of the schoolmaster or to project on to others his own shrink-

2. John 19:11.
3. *De Civitate Dei*, x. 12, 16, 24-26 and xix. 16.

ing from physical pain. His very altruism is selfish and — what matters more for the present argument — it does not avoid force; it avoids only one particularly unpleasant kind of force. To eliminate force altogether is not only to destroy the State, with all its potentialities for good, but to make human life as we have known it on the earth unlivable. Only a disembodied community could wholly eliminate bodily force.

This being so, it becomes important to see how this immense and terrible but necessary and inevitable thing can be controlled. For the recognition of power as essential in the life of the State does not mean the recognition of unlimited and uncontrolled power. Power and sovereignty are two different things. While we uphold the right use of the former, we may without inconsistency deplore the latter. We may even agree with Jacques Maritain that it would be a good thing if political philosophy could forget the name and even the conception of sovereignty.[4] As Bertrand de Jouvenel says, quoting Montesquieu: "All history shows that every man who has authority is led to abuse it; he does not stop until he comes up against limitations. It is a hard saying but limitations need to be set even to virtue herself."[5]

There is a school of thought, very popular in Africa today, and perhaps deriving its ultimate inspiration from Rousseau, which holds that any exercise of power is justified if only the tyranny is supported by universal suffrage. This is a mystique of humanity which forgets God and degrades man.[6] Nothing in all the long study of human history bears out the thesis that majorities are always right or even tolerable, that every majority decision is the considered will of the people, or that every election puts into office the General Will. The General

4. Jacques Maritain, *Man and the State* (Chicago: The University of Chicago Press, 1951), p. 24.
5. Bertrand de Jouvenel, *On Power* (New York: The Viking Press, 1949), p. 286.
6. See, e.g., Lord Percy of Newcastle, *The Heresy of Democracy* (Chicago: Henry Regnery Co., 1955).

Will of Rousseau is acceptable only in an idealized Swiss canton under exceptional conditions. But the marriage of the General Will to Leviathan, with Majority Vote as the witness to sign the register, is a portentous and unnatural alliance.

Let there be no mistake here. We do well to believe in national freedom. It is in the logic of history at this time. The colonial era is ended and ended irrevocably. We do well also to believe in universal suffrage — even the suffrage of the illiterate — because to refuse the vote to any man is a reflection on his humanity. No attack is directed against these, and therefore no defense of them is called for. What is attacked is the doctrine that universal suffrage will *in itself* put all things right, that universal suffrage will in some mysterious way be an adequate controller of its own force. We are back at the point which John Stuart Mill reached in the middle of last century — the point at which liberalism itself has to step in to protect individuals, each of infinite moral worth, from the tyranny of the majority.

Government without recourse to a majority vote seems to be impossible in the actual conditions of human life. So far it has proved impossible to find a satisfactory moral basis for majority rule: we can justify it only as a less disagreeable substitute for a fight. "We count heads instead of breaking them." Almost every great reform has been the work of an intelligent minority using enthusiasm and moral strength to obtain after many years the majority vote required to validate the reform. Of no movement is this statement more true than of the movements for national independence in Asia and Africa; but it is also a true description of the movements for the abolition of slavery and the emancipation of women. Let no one find a moral basis for majority rule whose religion calls on him to bow in worship before the tremendous and lonely minority of the Cross.

An acceptable alternative to majority rule would, if it were practicable, be government by consent. Over a couple of centuries the London Yearly Meeting of the Society of Friends has disposed of much important business and authorized the expenditure of large sums of money by this method without ever taking a majority vote. But can this example really be applied to the rough-and-ready politics of an ordinary state? The members of the Society of Friends are bound together by a common religious tradition and (one may hope) by some measure of brotherly charity. It may be unfortunate if a decision has to be deferred for lack of general agreement, but this does not paralyze the daily life of a great community, as would a failure to reach agreement by consent on the annual budget of the state.

If all men would at all times agree to work on the basis of general consent, it might be conceivable that force might be eliminated from the world and national affairs. But can men organized geographically, and not by common faith, commit themselves never to move forward without general consent? People do not join the Society of Friends without some acceptance of Quaker principles. If the London Yearly Meeting included Roman Catholics and Baptists, Episcopalians and Christian Scientists, atheists and agnostics, could it still do its business without ever having a majority vote?

To bring the spirit of consent into parliamentary business as far as possible would be a great boon. It would, for example, be of value if Select Committees were composed of equal numbers of Government and Opposition members, and were thus unable to report except by agreement. Napoleon's strange institutions of a *tribunat* which spoke but did not vote and a *corps législatif* which voted but did not speak would have had some value if the members of the *corps législatif* had really been quite open to being influenced by the *tribunat's* arguments — and if they had both not been so overshadowed by the Emperor and the Senate. The Fourth French Republic, for which history has had very little to say, did at least, through its institutions, make it possible for oratory and reasoning to influence votes. But it is only in very exceptional cases that a British or South African Member of Parliament can really feel that his speeches are going to influence the division, the nature of which can usually be predicted with considerable accuracy before the debate begins. The Member if in Opposition can produce irrefutable facts, convincing arguments, and pungent ridicule. But all in vain.

*He has his jest and they have his estate.*

It is this which makes parliamentary life frustrating to many modern parliamentarians, and especially so in countries where one party is deeply entrenched and no other really has a chance.

Practical political scientists would do a great service to humanity if they could find ways and means of checking majority rule by introducing elements of government by consent, and the fact that such government cannot be fully realized in the State as we know it ought not to prevent us from approximating to it as closely as we can. No political philosopher would claim that any state in history has ever achieved absolute justice, yet none would say that the State should not try to be as just as it can. Even love, which it is ludicrous to think of as fully embodied in political institutions, should be so sought after that kindness and caring may not be completely foreign to them.

Do what we will, however, majority rule will tend to be the normal rule of convenience in modern states, and since we cannot eliminate it we must seek for remedies to mitigate the tyranny of the majority.

Mill believed that one way of avoiding this was to educate the voters, and certainly any state introducing universal suffrage lays on itself the urgent duty of educating the voters, certainly for literacy, if possible for much more than literacy. However, education is a very broad term which needs analyzing and, while we accept Mill's argument, it is important to remember that one of the very worst tyrannies in human history, that of Adolf Hitler, was based on the vote of one of the best educated nations in the world, enjoying universal suffrage.

Plato believed in education, if possible even more than Mill. His faith that knowledge produced virtue would, if it could be substantiated by history and experience, make us believe that in good schools and universities we could find real protection against the tyranny of the majority. Alas! experience has shown very clearly in this twentieth century that, while schools and universities are undoubtedly a very powerful force, their power may be exercised for evil, supporting the very tyranny which they should check. Look where we will, the one sure safeguard of liberty is the loyalty and faith of individual human personalities and ultimately the Spirit of God in individual human lives.

But even if universities and schools were more reliable than they have shown themselves, we should still have to ask ourselves how the best men could be selected from among those who have passed through them, and, more deeply, whether government by the best men is the best form of government. Psychologists may be able to test intelligence, examiners (somewhat more doubtfully) acquired knowledge, but who shall test character? And who is fit to test character? *Quis custodiet ipsos custodes?*

Assume, however, that the best men are easily and infallibly discoverable, yet it must still be asked whether the government of the best men is desirable or acceptable in practice. We are trying, after all, to find a corrective to democracy, not a substitute for it. The tyranny of the majority is undesirable: is the remedy for it a tyranny of the minority, however good a minority? At least universal suffrage means that those who suffer from legislation have some opportunity of influencing those who make laws. And only they will know what laws in fact cause them discomfort or unhappiness.

We must therefore support John Stuart Mill's program for educating the masses and go on to consider his other remedies against the tyranny of the majority. One is the development of powerful and autonomous organs of local government, and with this we can be in hearty agreement, both because this is good in itself and also because powerful local government institutions are a check against an omnipotent central government. The federal principle operates as such a check, so within the component states of a federation does strong local government, so within all does the free individual. Mill desires passionately to safeguard within society that inner citadel of personality which makes the individual free. Mill's picture of the liberal state is virtually a federation of persons, and surely it is right that Hiram P. Smith has rights against the State of Massachusetts no less than the State of Massachusetts against the United States of America. Even a unitary State should be a federation of human personalities possessing some powers exclusive to themselves.

Before parting company with Mill, we should remember also his insistence on the value to individual freedom of private associations of men. This is a point which has been more fully developed in our own day by Jacques Maritain,[7] who has told us very clearly that the State is only one organ of society[8] and that the State is for man, not man for the State. The roaring, destructive torrent of power is to be turned into beneficent channels of irrigation small enough to be controlled by the people for whom they exist, for assuredly in nature power exists for man, not man for power.

Professor Cowen in his book *The Foundations of Freedom* has shown us the desirability of restricting power by law, and has discussed the effectiveness of controls such as those exercised by a rigid constitution and an entrenched bill of rights.[9]

7. Especially in *Man and the State*.
8. Or the "body politic" as he not very happily calls it.
9. D. V. Cowen, *The Foundations of Freedom* (Cape Town: Oxford University Press, 1961).

This restriction by law is one of the accepted controls of power, though not all-powerful in its effects, and it is sufficiently important to merit special discussion a little later.

Bertrand de Jouvenel in *On Power*,[10] and especially in *Sovereignty*,[11] has sought to recall holders of power to their moral obligations. In his view, with which we fully concur, the majority in a democracy requires just such instruction as was given to medieval princes in the *De Regimine Principum* and such inspiration for themselves as is found in St. Augustine's *Mirror of Princes*.[12] And surely we could apply St. Augustine's words to democratic leaders in Europe, Asia, or Africa: "Happy are they . . . if they make their power their trumpeter to divulge the true adoration of God's majesty; . . . if they long most for that empire where they may not fear to have partners; if they be slack to revenge, quick to forgive; if they use correction for the public good, not for private hate; . . . if they desire to rule their own desires rather than others' estates; and if they do all things not for glory but for charity." Surely Bertrand de Jouvenel is right when he feels that these are important lessons for any triumphant majority in a modern democracy, and that universal suffrage, if they are unlearned, is but dust and ashes. Surely Dr. Verwoerd or Dr. Nkrumah need these ideals no less than Theodosius or Justinian or Louis XIV. Mere democratic majority rule does not mean freedom without these strong moral strengths and restraints.

If power needs so much control even at its best, how deplorable must be the results of letting the desire to possess power for its own sake become the motive of political action. In some measure this temptation is to be found in every political career, just as dishonesty, in the view of the old Jewish philosopher, dogs every commercial transaction: "As a nail

---

10. New York: The Viking Press, 1949.
11. London: Cambridge University Press, 1957.
12. *De Civitate Dei*, v. 24.

sticketh fast between the joinings of the stones, so doth sin stick close between buying and selling."[13] A few exceptional men seem to be exempt from it, as apparently was Robert E. Lee: many succeed in conquering and taming it, as did Abraham Lincoln. Others are possessed by it, some consciously (and they are the less dangerous), others unconsciously. What makes it so insidious an enemy is that it is often a development of genuine patriotic feeling. When the Afrikaner Broederbond was formed in South Africa by a small group of Nationalists, there were real grievances to be redressed and real ideals, however limited, to be realized. There was much to be said for a movement aimed at giving Afrikaners a bigger status in the land of their birth. Even at this stage the Broederbond began to go in the wrong direction because of its desire to give Afrikaners greater power rather than greater opportunity of service. Now that the Republic of South Africa is in being and almost every important post in it is held by an Afrikaner, any continuance of the activities of the Broederbond can only be motivated by the growth of a love of power for its own sake. This twisting to evil of a good motive is a common phenomenon of movements for national independence. Africa in particular has during the last decade seen many Nationalist movements beginning with something of a genuine desire for freedom and maturity twisted to support the power of a party or of a single man. It is one of the greatest achievements of India, due to the saintliness of Gandhi and the more secular integrity of Nehru, that the Indian independence movement has not thus degenerated. In Africa there has been a tradition of personal rule; and, with political leadership replacing chieftainship, this militates against real democratic freedom, as does the *caudillo* principle in parts of Latin America. Nor is it confined to black Africa, for in the Republic of South Africa men have often tended to follow leaders rather than principles. "I am a Smuts

13. Ecclus. 27:2.

man" used to be a by no means unusual remark, and dissentient Nationalism is too often seen as disloyalty to Dr.
Verwoerd.

Power cannot be eliminated from politics. A desire to
serve one's country in public life is inevitably a desire to
exercise power, even if this is disclaimed, even if it is genu-
inely a mere by-product of public spirit. But allow power to
become a motive, and childish madness supervenes — the kind
of madness that will break down the containing walls in order
to have the thrill of seeing a great rush of "waters unwith-
stood" flooding the countryside. Power is useful, power is
legitimate, power is natural, power is of God, but always as
an ancillary. When it is sought for its own sake it is an utter
curse both to those wielding it and to those subject to it.

Even as an ancillary it must be put under strong moral restraints. Two of the greatest defenders of uncontrolled power
had as their ultimate aim something different from power —
Machiavelli, the union of Italy, Hobbes, security in a very
troubled world. But the end, even if good, does not justify
the use of unbridled power as a means.

To some natures the temptation takes a different form.
Men are content to be *éminences grises,* powers behind the
throne. Such may be the temptation of a white man in tropi-
cal Africa, forever banned from the direct exercise of power,
even from benevolent paternalism, but hopeful of exercising
avuncular influence and thus secretly glorifying his own
personality. Even at this early stage of our study we are being
led to the conclusion that the primal sin of substituting the
ego for God, of separating self from the essential unity of
which it should be a part, is the enemy to be conquered, and
by what power can so strong and insidious an enemy be overcome?

The State is the ultimate repository, more than any other
institution, of man's power, of the physical strength of organized humanity. In its use of physical force it is almost

unique; in its possession of unlimited physical force it is unique. How great, therefore, the need to put this immense potential destroyer under control, spiritual, moral, and legal. "The increase of the State's power," says Bertrand de Jouvenel, "has been paralleled by the increase of the power of the human race for deadly mischief."[14] There is no doubt that this is true. There is also no doubt that man could not if he would, and would not if he could, take the inventive genius out of his mind or the skill out of his fingers. It may be used for evil, but if man is unable to do evil he will be equally unable to do good. Therefore the only political way out of the human dilemma as seen by De Jouvenel is to limit the power of the State.

We begin by considering control by law. Law is fully as old in human history as power. There is even a case for saying that law is older — that law controlled the daily life of human beings before their resources were marshaled to enforce it. We know of no human group, however "primitive," which has not the control of law written in its heart and into its institutions. The law may appear to us to be rudimentary. Much of it may appear to consist of tribal "taboos" (which, however, are among the most effective known restraints on human action), but everywhere there is also the beginning of a conscience, the deep if not clear realization that certain things are ultimately right and others ultimately wrong.

Modern ideas of law, especially those influenced by British practice, tend to associate it with the action of the legislature in the exercise of its sovereign power. This is to make law the creature of power rather than a restraint on it. We shall recur to this point later, but in the meantime we must note that this is a very recent conception of law and would have seemed strange indeed to men in most of the long centuries of human history. Assuredly to both Plato and Aristotle law was something superior to mortal men and not created by

14. In the preface to *On Power*.

them, and if the Romans taught that "what pleases the prince has the force of law," they none the less re-created Roman law by basing the *ius gentium* not on what they enacted but on what they found. The *ius gentium* rested on what the *praetor peregrinus* considered to be the principles on which he ought to base his administration of justice for the forthcoming year, not on any enactment of emperor, senate, or people. It was on the *ius gentium* that the great legal instruments of later ages, such as the Code of Justinian, rested. The emperors had become autocrats, but the law was above them. The law of nature, the law of right reason, the basis of the conduct of the reasonable man, flowed from the same source — the observation of and reflection upon the principles of law discovered among the nations of the world — and not on legislation.

Such was the view of law, Germanic as well as Roman, during the Middle Ages. Law was a thing to be discovered and reverenced, not made. In St. Thomas Aquinas' wonderful and profound study of law, human law is made subject to eternal, natural, and divine law; but even human law as he saw it was in the main something which had grown up in the life of a kingdom, not the will of a king. To be sure there were always exceptional pieces of legislation, but they were the exception rather than the rule. In South Africa who enacted Roman-Dutch law or Zulu tribal law? There were statutes which recognized these systems of law, but they no more created them than they created the seasons.

From time to time there have arisen among human beings men who were great legislators, men who strove to turn their will or even their whim into law, such men as Napoleon, or Hitler, or Shaka. Even at their worst, men of this kind left certain rules of law untouched, and so great was the prestige of law that they tried to express their arbitrary will in legal guise, giving it the *form* of law, in order that it might acquire some of the sanctity due to the *reality* of law. A man like Shaka, the founder of the Zulu nation in Napoleon's day (who, of course, is no more representative of Bantu conceptions of government than Hitler was of European conceptions of government), could go very far in defying age-long custom, but even he had to leave the Zulu family system intact, and to refrain from touching the law of succession and the legal position of women relative to their male guardians.

All this brings us up to the theory of the law of nature. Ultimately international law rests on this theory. When Grotius sought to stem the international anarchy of the seventeenth century he sought once again to discover law, and even when in fact he legislated he did so in the guise of discovering legal principles.

The law of nature is that which right reason shows the ordinary man to be fair. No special religious revelation, no enactment of a sovereign prince, is needed to tell the average man that *pacta sunt servanda,* that contracts entered into without fraud or force are to be kept. He knows that to be true and to be binding upon the State in the exercise of its great but not unlimited power.

The conception of the law of nature is often challenged nowadays. Its challengers are not always consistent. Some of them appear to favor very greatly the supreme document which the law of nature has produced — the United Nations Declaration of Human Rights.

Critics of the law of nature deny that there can be any such thing as absolute ethics, as from a different standpoint does St. Augustine with his *"Dilige et quod vis fac."* They feel that the law of nature is an attempt to clothe morality in a legal form, but surely it is much more important to stress the close connection between law and morality than to separate them. With greater plausibility they point out that the rules of the law of nature apply only to "civilized man" and quote cases like the head-hunters of Borneo to show that among "savage" nations the rules of the law of nature do not apply.

But though we should not sanction head-hunting in Western Europe, at any rate in peacetime, we must remember that even in Borneo certain heads could not be hunted, namely the heads of the hunter's fellow-tribesmen. Even there life was never placed at the mercy of man's mere whim. Western Europe has in general aways admitted some exceptions to the rule "Thou shalt not kill." In Borneo the exceptions are more numerous but the fundamental rule is the same. The sexual practices of the Australian aboriginal seem loose in the extreme to the European research worker, but examination will show that although the limits of permissible action are much wider than in Europe, yet there are limits and within them the law is stringently applied. In old Zulu custom external sexual intercourse between boys and girls was tolerated and almost approved, but penetration resulting in pregnancy was most sternly disapproved and punished. Nowhere in the whole history of the world has there ever been a society which tolerated complete sexual promiscuity. However strangely the law varied, there was always a law of some kind which restrained men's actions.

The majestic peak of natural law is unchanging, but men approaching it from different directions may give a different account of it. The picture drawn by someone nearer may differ from that sketched further away, but the mountain itself does not change.

Deeply written, then, in the heart of mankind, is this conception of law as something without which power is intolerable. It is only in very recent decades that the misleading conception of law as the expression of the sovereign's will has opened the door to the use of arbitrary power made to look less wicked by being clothed with the form, though not the reality, of law.

The Constitution of the United States shows the way in which the ancient conception of the supremacy of law can be formalized in the modern state. But all constitutional safeguards of this kind must depend ultimately on the reverence for law in the community. This must be a reverence for the principles of right, not for a so-called "law" or statute which outrages them. South Africans do have a muddled respect for law so great that arbitrary action has to be based on the authority of a statute to be fully acceptable. Thus it is not merely a respect for law that is needed, but a greater understanding of what law really means. Even here the fundamental remedies are educational and spiritual. Let us remember this as our study progresses.

The South African respect for so-called "law" — statutes legalizing the unrighteous — may be contrasted with Plato's respect for right. Plato, as we all know, began by believing in the government of the best men, men to whom education had brought virtue. His motto might well have been *Disce, et quod vis fac,* as eight centuries later St. Augustine's was *Dilige et quod vis fac.* A lifetime's experience brought him to believe that for the affairs of state the sure and impersonal rule of law was more practicable than the glorious and unpredictable decisions of the philosopher-kings. It was not a mere formal law that he was thinking about, for the philosopher-kings could after all have enacted statutes to give their inspirations a legal form: it was law springing from what had been thought to be right and had found a home in the immemorial customs of the people. And when Socrates in the *Crito* brings in the laws of Athens to argue with him and convince him of his duty to stay in Athens and die, it was the whole body of law of Athens of which he was thinking, not some statute passed by the Ecclesia to meet his or any other particular situation.

Far other was the interpretation of law in the South African constitutional crisis of 1951-1956. Since the details of this crisis are not known as well as they should be outside the Republic, let us recapitulate them here.

In 1852, the Cape of Good Hope Constitution Ordinance conferred the franchise on all the people of the Cape, without distinction of race or color, who conformed to certain minimum educational and property qualifications. These qualifications were subsequently raised, but they remained nonracial throughout the history of the old Cape Colony, and political leaders of both white groups sought for and obtained the votes of Colored men, nor did they challenge the principle of non-racial franchise.

When in 1908 and 1909 the National Convention set to work to create out of the four colonies the Union of South Africa the question of the political rights of non-white South Africans was one of the most formidable difficulties of the founding fathers. The statesmen of the Cape Colony were not prepared to barter these rights away. No one party, no one racial group, monopolized this attitude. Among its foremost protagonists were Afrikaners such as J. H. Hofmeyr ("Onze Jan"), J. W. Sauer, and F. S. Malan. The fiction has been sedulously spread that it was pressure from the British government which secured the entrenchment of Colored political rights in the South Africa Act. The pressure came not from the British government, but from fellow-statesmen and fellow-Afrikaners in the Cape Colony. It is fair to say that but for the entrenchment of Colored voting rights in the Cape Province there would have been no Union. Even if the pressure had come from the British government, it would still have been part of the bargain of Union. A great benefit had been conferred on South Africa at a small cost, and this contract was freely entered into by the statesmen of all four colonies of South Africa without fraud or force. It is indubitable that this was a case where *pacta sunt servanda*. To evade the obligations of this contract while retaining its benefits was against the law of nature, and what purported to be legislation was, in view of its conflict with true justice, not law in the deepest and truest sense of that term.

The South Africa Act, while leaving the Parliament of South Africa free to amend the Constitution as a whole, en-

trenched non-white voting rights in the Cape by demanding
that Parliament should sit unicamerally and that not less
than two-thirds of the total number of members of both
houses should vote in favor of any interference with these
rights.

In 1931 the Statute of Westminster conferred sovereign independence on South Africa. Its provisions were incorporated
in the Status Act passed by the South African Parliament in
1934. The most categorical assurances were given by ministers
who afterward supported all the trickery of the period 1951-
1956 that, whatever legal interpretation might be given to
the Statute of Westminster and the Status Act, the restrictions
laid down by the Constitution would, as a matter of conscience, honor, and morality, be honored in letter and in
spirit. A few years later these assurances were repudiated, and
this must be looked on, if ethics may be given any meaning
at all, as dishonorable and immoral.

When in 1936 General Hertzog wished to take Africans off
the ordinary voters' rolls and place them on a separate community roll returning a limited number of members of Parliament, he, notwithstanding the Statute of Westminster and
the Status Act, followed in every detail the procedure pre-
scribed by the Constitution. He obtained his two-thirds majority. In fact he waited ten years — his first legislation having been introduced in 1926 — in order to get it by fair means.
His action was politically unwise and wrong, and based on
wrong premises, but was not a breach of contract.

In 1951 the government introduced legislation to follow a
similar course with the "Colored" people[15] — to place them
in their turn on a separate community roll, returning a
limited number of members of Parliament, instead of leaving them on the common roll where they had been for ninety-
nine years. Realizing that it was politically impossible to get
the requisite two-thirds majority, the government introduced

15. I.e., people of mixed race.

legislation and carried it through each of the Houses of Parliament separately by simple majorities.[16]

An act of political spoliation which was at the same time a breach of faith was thus clothed with the diaphanous texture of an act of Parliament. Power was thus inadequately covered by "law." Observe that no South African statesman would have dared to take away a fundamental right merely by his own arbitrary whim. The reverence for law cherished for many generations had to be appeased by a document which looked like a law. Hypocrisy in this instance was the homage paid by vice to virtue.

The law courts would have none of it. The Appellate Division of the South African Supreme Court held in 1952 that the document of 1951 was not a "law" at all, even in the most limited sense of the term "law." It was not a valid statute. The very existence and functioning of Parliament was based on the same Constitution the provisions of which Parliament had chosen to ignore in the case before us.

The government rejoined by carrying through Parliament, sitting bicamerally and by simple majorities in each house, another "law" which converted the legislature into a "High Court of Parliament" empowered to adjudicate in constitutional cases. It summoned this so-called "High Court," from which almost all those members of Parliament who were not government supporters stayed away, and received from it the expected "validation" of its original act.

But again appeal was made to the Appellate Division of the Supreme Court and again the unlawful action of Parliament was invalidated. The so-called "High Court of Parliament" had been judge in its own case, and no more flagrant violation of the law of nature than this could be imagined. Yet it took the form of "law" and the force of the majority validat-

16. For details and references, see Cowen, *The Foundations of Freedom,* chap. iii. I am greatly indebted to Professor Cowen for his clear and comprehensive survey of the whole constitutional crisis.

ing its own actions was given the outward appearance of a court of law.

Thus foiled for a second time, the government persuaded Parliament to enact two further pieces of legislation. The first of these acts enabled the government to add six judges to the five-judge Appellate Division of the Supreme Court when it sat to adjudicate constitutional issues. That it was not necessary to use this power does not alter the fact that it was an inroad of a most deplorable kind into the independence of the law courts and the sanctity of law.

The second of these acts — the Senate Act of 1955 — reconstituted the South African Senate with great ingenuity, in such a way that combined with the House of Assembly it would provide the government with the support of two-thirds of the total number of members in a joint sitting of the two houses. This was to pack Parliament, but it was not in direct contravention of the Constitution. It involved the abolition of the principle of the equal representation of the provinces in the Senate, the abolition of the principle of electing senators by the system of proportional representation, and the doubling of the number of senators nominated by the government.

Parliament met in 1956 with a Senate so reconstituted. A joint sitting of the two houses was called, the necessary majority of two-thirds of the total number of members of both houses obtained, and the disfranchisement measure at last carried. Once again appeal was made to the Appellate Division of the Supreme Court, but the Court, with one dissentient voice — that of Mr. Justice Schreiner — now held that Colored voters had been lawfully removed from the voters' roll.

At this stage the "law" had attained a formal validity: it was no longer in conflict with the letter of the Constitution. But everybody knew that this had been obtained by a clever trick. The fundamental issues were unchanged. A "law," valid in form, had enacted a grave injustice. The South African voters as a whole were, however, satisfied, because the injustice had been done by "legal" means.

It is not claimed here that the South African Parliament has not the power, like the British Parliament, to enact what it will — in the South African case subject to its formal compliance with the procedures laid down for the amendment of the rigid clauses in its Constitution. But between a "law" that is a law only because it is a formal act of power by a sovereign legislature and a law that is a law because it is essentially just and not in conflict with the law of nature there is a great gulf fixed, and the attitude to be attacked is that which gives to the former the sanctity which belongs only to the latter, for this is to crown power with the name of law, not to call in law to control power.

It is regrettable that the British doctrine of the sovereignty of Parliament has been accepted as part of the fundamental law of South Africa. It is — if one may risk so notable a heresy — of doubtful value in Britain itself. If, however, so dangerous a principle is to be transplanted elsewhere, it must be accompanied by the traditions and conventions which alone make it bearable even in a homogeneous country where every adult is a voter. Time alone can build up the traditions; the sensitive conventions of fair play find it hard to survive under the scorching wind of dynamic nationalism. While in England the law courts are unable to question the validity of an act of Parliament, it is customary[17] to use the condemnatory term "unconstitutional" for acts which are in fact unjust in their content or the methods of enacting which are questionable.

The issues must be put again and again until they are plain to us all, that law is the natural check against power; that law which is really *ars aequi et boni* is entitled to deep reverence;

17. A. V. Dicey, *Law of the Constitution* (London: Macmillan and Co., 1897), Appendix vii.

that so-called "law" which is merely a cloak for power is not really law at all; that, finally, it is preposterous to ask for reverence for such "law" as if it were true law, or to demand obedience to it as a Christian duty. Otherwise we find ourselves involuntarily assenting to the definition of Thrasymachus that justice is the interest of the stronger.

Were it otherwise we should have to bespeak the reverence of men for the tyranny and murder of Hitler, who also (so strange is man) hesitated to say merely "This man must be killed because I do not like him," but covered himself with the legal powers conferred on him by an obsequious Reichstag. We should have had to defend Stalin's purges, because Stalin could always, under the curious constitution of 1936, obtain the unanimous support of the All-Union Soviet for any action which he took. In English history we should have to justify the worst excesses of Henry VIII because he acted under the authority of the disgraceful *lex regia* which his subservient Parliament was induced to pass.

It is important that men, whether in Africa or elsewhere, should recognize these truths. In the wider Africa, where modern forms of the doctrines of Rousseau and Marx have such considerable sway, it is time to stress the fundamentals of that political philosophy that runs like a golden thread through human history — the political philosophy of Plato and Aristotle, of Cicero and the great Roman jurists, of St. Augustine and St. Thomas Aquinas, of Hooker and Grotius, of Locke and Mill, of D'Entrèves and De Jouvenel and Maritain. It is not enough to give everyone the vote, for, right and inspiring though this is, it is not the whole of liberty: it was under a constitution which gave every man and woman over twenty in Germany the vote that Hitler came into power. It is not enough to remove economic inequalities if men are left in a position of personal degradation before an all-powerful State.

Even those who are most devoted to the doctrine that the

vote is everything show their secret and deep hopes and fears by throwing the cloak of "legality" over their tyrannical actions. Nothing that Dr. Nkrumah has done to his Opposition is not covered by some act of the legislature, normal or retrospective. Here is a vague recognition of the place of law coupled with actions which take from it all its meaning.

In conclusion, may we accept two simple propositions, viz.:

*1.* Power to be tolerable needs to be controlled by law, and this is one of the deepest and oldest convictions of the human race.

*2.* Law, if it is to control power, may not be defined merely as the will of him who holds the power, but must rest on fundamental principles of justice, acceptable to the human heart at its best.

*Chapter Two*

## RIGHT AND LOVE

We have seen how important it is not to get confused by the different meanings of the term "law," nor to give to a statute which is a mere emanation of power the reverence which is due only to the true principles of law based on right. It is one of the ambiguities of the English language that "law" can be used in these widely differing senses. To make the argument clear, let us speak of "right." We may get law and power mixed up in our minds, but never power and right.

The true check on power, therefore, is right, and this enables us to withstand the sophistries that defend wrong because it has been thrown into the form of a statute. Without that justice which is the exercise of authority in the maintenance of right the State has no moral authority at all. *"Remota iustitia, quid sunt regna nisi magna latrocinia?"* St. Augustine speaks the truth when he says this. The immense power of the State used unjustly is no better than organized robbery.

What then is right and how can we define its content? The old Roman jurists very nearly identified the universal practice of law (*ius gentium*) with ideal reason (the law of nature, *ius naturale*), but the existence of one institution which was universally practiced but could never be approved by right reason prevented this confusion of thought. That institution was slavery. Slavery was recognized in the *ius gentium,* but never given even a foothold in the realm of the law of nature. Here, then, is a beginning. Slavery and justice are irreconcilable.

Slavery is surely condemned not because of any legal anomalies about it, nor because of the frequent occurrence of cruelty within the system, for though slavery is often brutal it need not be so. Slavery is condemned because it makes one human personality completely subservient to another human personality. Man, who is an end in himself, is made a means to an end.

If this is the real reason for the condemnation of slavery, we have a clear indication of the essential criterion of what is just and what is unjust. That is unjust which fails to respect personality.

There is a field of study which needs to be explored much more than it ever has been. All over Asia and Africa during the past century recognition has been given by white rulers to indigenous legal systems, "in so far as they are compatible with humanity," "in so far as they are not inconsistent with the general principles of humanity observed throughout the civilized world." The phrase varies from territory to territory, but it is obvious that recognition is refused to injustice while it is not refused to widely differing legal systems.

What in fact has been refused? All, in particular, that degrades women below the level of free and independent personality. However much marriage is in African law a transaction between family and family, not between individual and individual, however much it is regularized by the unfamiliar institution of the bride-price, the woman's consent must now be publicly given: she may not be coerced. In the same way in Asia the law has refused to countenance child marriage and the custom of *suttee*. A woman is a person, in the deepest sense an equal person, and law which conforms with right must respect her as such.

It is clear that this thought, carried to its logical conclusion, must condemn as inconsistent with right and justice all restrictions based on race and color that have the effect of degrading the person of color and denying his full humanity.

Were the United Nations to recognize the law of South Africa "in so far as it is not inconsistent with the general principles of humanity observed throughout the civilized world" it would have to reject the color bar, just as South African jurists in recognizing Zulu and Xhosa law have rejected witchcraft. It is not only the color bar that is at stake, important though this undoubtedly is. It is fundamental human values, the basis of all political philosophy. It is that liberty which John Stuart Mill defended so ardently. His division of human activities into self-regarding and other-regarding acts may be logically unsatisfying, but it is groping after a great truth — the truth that in each man there is an inner citadel of personality into which the State has no right to enter.

We recognize the difficulties. It is not easy to make exhaustive, clear-cut lists of self-regarding and other-regarding actions. But neither is it easy to make completely satisfactory lists of exclusive federal powers and exclusive state powers in a federation, yet federations work, they serve a useful purpose, and their success defies logic. The fact that there are exclusive state powers is vital to federal government. States accept association on this basis and no other. As Neuchâtel and Zug, as Vermont and Georgia, as Nova Scotia and Quebec, as New South Wales and Western Australia preserve personalities recognizably different both from each other and from the federal whole, so provision should be made in the State for individual personalities, and that provision demands something like a list of exclusive personal rights. A free state must be, in short, a federation of free persons, secure in their personality. There must be spheres of life in which the State cannot intervene. This is liberty.

The other side of justice is the promotion of truth. With this in view mankind has built up across the centuries a legal procedure designed to sift truth from falsehood and, without personal bias, to defend truth that it may prevail.

The law court, as we know it, is a sacrament of justice — "a means whereby we receive the same and a pledge to assure us thereof." By a strange paradox it is, and must be, impersonal in its defense of personality. It must operate in public that all men may see that justice is being done. It must make available the services of professional men, trained to honor justice and its procedures.[1] It must have a procedure that sifts every piece of evidence thoroughly and protects the truth at all points. It must prevent any man from being judge in his own cause. It must see that both sides are heard. It must use neither force nor bribery. The lawyer who betrays these principles is a disloyal servant of justice. The statesman who does not make them his basis of government becomes the foe of freedom, the enemy of truth, and the destroyer of personality.

For these rules of the law court call for a wider application in the whole field of government. The defense of personal freedom needs, as we have seen, an impersonal adjudicator. That is why the law courts, with their long tradition of impersonal austerity, ought to be the protectors of private rights. Executive officers have not the same training and do not work in the same atmosphere. Even civil servants cannot be trusted to be completely impartial in matters where sentiment can easily be roused. Take, for example, the procedure for racial classification in South Africa. On the correctness of this classification lies in that distressed country much of the personal happiness of the person classified. When (as has not infrequently happened) one who has been considered as white is classified as "colored,"[2] he is in the gravest danger of losing his job, his children suffer the shattering experience of being moved from a superior white school to an inferior "colored" school, he becomes subject to all the segregation laws as re-

1. In tribal society, professional men are replaced by the chief's uncles, other old and experienced men, and men whom experience has shown to be skilful in these matters.
2. I.e., of mixed race.

gards railway travel, attendance at entertainments, and the like, and if he is engaged to a girl who is classified as white, his marriage becomes impossible in view of the Mixed Marriages Act. When (as happens less frequently) a person who has been considered as "colored" is classified as "Native," he must carry a pass, live in a "location," be subjected to the influx control laws, and see the degradation of himself and his children in being moved to a yet lower social caste. Obviously the fundamental remedy is to remove this inhuman color bar. But while it exists surely this nauseous business of "classification" should, in view of all that is entailed in it, be put into the hands of professional judges, trained by long practice to handle as impersonally as possible and with courtesy, even if it is an austere courtesy, the human beings concerned, who, on the contrary, are dealt with by civil servants, behind closed doors, men with only an imperfect tradition of impersonal impartiality and often lacking in courtesy.

We have spoken of "closed doors" and here it must be said that publicity is the life-blood of freedom. Internments in wartime are an example of the injustice which is bred by secrecy. It is hard to believe that, even during hostilities, they do not do more harm than good. Certainly similar procedures in peacetime are dangerous and unjust. In South Africa, again, the Suppression of Communism Act places any individual whom the government dislikes at the mercy of a political minister, no one hearing the accusation, the accused's defense, or the reasons for the minister's decision. Strange these must be when one considers the case of a Cape Town journalist, famous for his hostility to Communism, "deemed to be a Communist" by the minister, presumably because he is a liberal of radical views opposed to the color bar.

It is not only in quasi-judicial decisions that this principle of publicity matters. If justice has as one of its aims the vindication of truth, it is important that the people should have full access to all the arguments for and against any proposed course of action. The same love for truth which makes a court insist on hearing fully and publicly the case for the defense as well as the prosecution should operate in all political controversy. Freedom of speech, freedom of public meeting, freedom of the press all operate to enable an intelligent democracy to make up its own mind. *Magna est veritas et praevalebit.* When truth is not given free course, justice is not done. When men are afraid of truth, liberties are lost, democracy degenerates into a police state, and the air becomes heavy-laden with fear.

In a court of law properly constituted, the plaintiff and the defendant are alike entitled, and indeed encouraged, to be represented by trained professional men. Subject to the right of the judge to intervene in order to check abuses, these men may cross-examine witnesses fully, and if need be severely, and unless the judge so permits no one may refuse to answer questions because they are awkward or inconvenient. Here, again, the law courts are a sacrament of right in the wider sphere of state life. A state is in danger when a government can, as in Ghana, persistently silence opposition: it is as though the counsel for the prosecution had the power to send the counsel for the defense to jail whenever his cross-examination became a nuisance. In Parliament, Government and Opposition alike serve the State. The English usage of referring to the Opposition as "Her Majesty's Opposition" puts matters in perspective. An Opposition may be factious and unreasonable, but even at its worst it is the servant of truth, for an unopposed Government twists and suppresses truth as surely as night follows day.

No principle of law is more clearly established than the principle that a man may not be judge in his own cause. This is undoubtedly a part of the law of nature and will be accepted as law without hesitation even in the courts of those countries in which it is not fashionable to speak of the law of nature. It seems so elementary a rule of justice. All of us accept it almost instinctively and hold to it in the depth of our being. We may recollect the pathetic little poem in *Alice in Wonderland:*

> *Fury said to a mouse,*
> *That he met in the house,*
> *Let us both go to law:*
> *I will prosecute you.*
> *Come, I'll take no denial;*
> *We must have a trial . . .*
> *I'll be judge, I'll be jury,*
> *Said cunning old Fury,*
> *I'll try the whole cause*
> *And condemn you to death.*

In the Republic of South Africa, a grimmer Wonderland than Alice ever knew, Fury is replaced by the white man and the mouse by the Indian trader or the Colored resident in a desirable suburb. The Group Areas Act[3] has as its object the residential separation of the different racial or color groups in the Republic. The whole basis of the legislation is race, as that term is used in South Africa; hence it is not unfair to consider its administration in terms of race. And here the striking fact is that, without a single exception, every public body charged with the duty of allocating areas to the different races is composed solely of white men. It is white men and white men only who decide what areas in a certain town shall be available for white men and what for men who are not white. Is it surprising that in every case the white population gets the best areas? It is as though a father's farm fell to be divided between two sons, and the elder was both charged with the duty of dividing it up and also given the first pick. Is there any place for truth or justice in such a setup?

It adds to the indignity and unworthiness of it all that these inequitable divisions are made by bodies that copy the

3. Or rather Acts, for it is a maze of amended and re-amended legislation.

procedure of courts of law and solemnly hear evidence, so that justice itself is brought into disrepute by a pretense that ends so uniformly in injustice.

In a court of law, properly so called, there is no place for either force or bribery. It is to prevent even the indirect use of force against justice that judges hold their positions, in the old phrase, *quamdiu se bene gesserint*. In every sphere of state life this ought to be the case. Wherever the life or liberty of opponents of the government is threatened, force intervenes to prevent the democracy which is the collective judge from knowing the truth and acting on it. Here again Ghana is a sad example.

The question of bribery is one which may well affect any democracy, however it may be free in other respects. Whenever the electorate, or sections of it, are appealed to on the basis of interest, whenever taxes are reduced just before an election, truth suffers and righteousness suffers. It may be complained that this is setting too high an ideal for sinful man; but justice *is* an ideal, and we must try to live up to it.

> *The gods are just and of our pleasant vices*
> *Make instruments to plague us.*

We may go on with our quotation:

> *The dark and vicious place where thee he got*
> *Cost him his eyes.*

For a bribed electorate loses the power to see straight. Its "pleasant vices" cut it off from the light of truth.

Right, then, we have seen, consists of a deep respect for personality, combined with a free love of truth. This is that justice by which every so-called "law" is to be tested. It will be claimed by some that justice matters little by the side of love. But justice is a valid thing. Love comes not to destroy but to fulfil. We may remember Who it was who said,

"Blessed are they that do hunger and thirst after justice,"[4] when we are tempted to relegate justice to too low a place in the scheme of things.

I do not wish to shirk the great difficulties which have to be met if we take this exalted view of justice. No wonder some men think that there is no such thing as absolute right. The picture of an ideal court given earlier in this chapter seems little like reality as we consider a People's Court in Soviet Russia engaged in liquidating a "deviationist." Communism as it is at present does not harmonize with either aspect of right as presented here. Individual personality is not sacrosanct if it is in conflict with the Party. Truth is not a virtue, is indeed not truth, if it harms the Cause. Communism has held the reins of government for less than half-a-century, a relatively short time in the history of thought. In its insistence on economic equality and its zeal for education it shows in its own way some care for such persons as are willing to conform to its creed. Nevertheless, there are insuperable difficulties in reconciling it with the picture of justice given here.

The faults of South Africa are easily seen, and while she is impenitent it is just to emphasize them. In another way the conflict of Communism with ideal justice is obvious and must be stressed. But in every country men fall short of the ideal, and the temptation to say that all morality is relative, a thing of particular times and places, is very strong. Is it reasonable, facing these facts, to argue that there is such a thing as absolute ethics? On what basis can this doctrine be maintained? Is the law of nature any more than a faded dream of the Classical and Middle Ages?

As we face these disturbing questions, we realize their strength and the difficulty of answering them; yet at the same time we feel deeply that the conception of right set out in this chapter is valid and true, that truth has a meaning apart from

4. Or "righteousness": it is the same word in Greek.

its relevance to any cause that we have at heart, that respect for personality is not merely a question of giving a man economic advancement and education, that freedom is an absolute value which is demanded by the very nature of man.

We may rest our case on the long history of mankind, arguing that the present aspect of Communism is a passing error which the next couple of centuries will put right. We may also say that the existence of sin does not invalidate the conception of virtue, that endemic injustice does not mean that justice is an illusion. Does the prevalence of adultery mean that fidelity is no longer a virtue? Does a cholera epidemic prove that there is no such thing as health?

But in the end we are driven to say that our faith in right *is* fundamentally an act of faith. To those who have the quaint idea that faith is the ability to believe unreasonable things this will have little meaning. But, happily, there are those who go deeper. Faith is not unreasonable. Faith is the leap into the unknown when reason can take men no further. All life worth living is based on it. Marriage and the begetting of children, unless they are to be degraded to the mere inevitable satisfaction of biological urges, represent acts of practical faith of the very highest order and the very greatest importance. Without faith life cannot really be lived at all. The man never existed who could give logical answers to every objection that anyone might raise to what he knows in his bones to be the right course of action. I do not speak here of specifically religious faith. This I should like to discuss later. I speak of that faith which is the assumption of every man of action, that creed which is not what a man feels he ought to believe but rather that which he knows he must believe or perish.

In the light and warmth of this faith, let us take a firm stand for right. Let us honor right as it frees and defends human personality. Let us rejoice that over the centuries slaves have been freed, and respect paid more and more to those who, without special privilege, education, or genius, are yet men. Let us rejoice that we have striven increasingly since

1789 for liberty and equality, and now fraternity. Let us rejoice in the steady liberation of women. Let us have thankful hearts that our own century has seen such great advances in respect to the personality of children. We know that this, like every good cause, has been hindered by sentimentalists, extremists, and cranks. But sentimentalists at least feel, even if their feelings get a little twisted; extremists alone enable moderate people to feel of importance; and a crank is what society must use in the absence of a self-starter. Let us rejoice, especially, that we have lived to see the great beginnings of the conquest of race prejudice. Let us be glad that the principles of right forbid us to limit any human life or personality by restrictions based on race or color. "Bliss is it in this dawn to be alive." Let those who live in countries like South Africa not be daunted by the fierce anger of those around them who defend color restrictions, for these are defending a doomed injustice. Whatever we personally have to dare and bear, we can be glad that this great burden is being lifted from the shoulders of tens of millions of our fellow-men. Surely if ever the morning stars sing together and all the sons of God shout for joy it is when brave men, men of faith, open the gates of freedom, break the chains, take a step in history from which there is no drawing back.

No less joyful is it to be the servants of truth, to fight every restriction on freedom of thought, speech, and writing, to let the search for truth carry us where it will, to let no preconceived assumptions be roadblocks in our journey. Is there any more exhilarating freedom than this willingness to follow truth where it leads? Not that old beliefs are always wrong; they are often deeply right, but they must be seen in the context of new experiences and needs. The attempt to protect them destroys them. Truth lives in freedom and faith.

All power is dangerous unless it is controlled by right. The power of the State, inevitable and not immoral, can become a raging peril, unless right, and not mere law, limits its exercise. Right, righteousness, justice — use whichever term you

prefer — is the fact which can make power a blessing. Therefore let this great thing which we find in us at our best, and
which is yet beyond us as well as in us, receive the best
panegyrics which we can offer, and let us demand that the
word "law" if it is to be used to invoke our obedience must be
impregnated with this which alone can give it a moral value.
The path of right is in itself valid and in itself entitled to
claim our hearts' obedience and the loyalty of our wills.

*But yet I show unto you a more excellent way.*

Picture a child brought up in a righteous home, handled
in every aspect of life with inflexible justice, but denied love.
What could ever make up for that aridity?

We know the difference better than we can define it. Considered deeply, justice is not ever complete justice without
love, and love not based on righteousness is not true love.
Yet there is a difference and we know it. The absence of love
makes life intolerable. An occasional injustice can be borne
if we are sure of love underneath.

If we come to consider it, the deep content of love is not
essentially different from that of right as we have defined it
earlier in this chapter. Love, too, means respect for personality. Love, too, must be based on truth and must live in freedom. Love is the fulfilling of the law, not its destruction.

To define the difference between the two is not easy, for it
is a difference of spirit rather than of content. In such a case
we may turn to a poetic picture for that which is so hard to
express in prose, and quote the sestet from the fourth sonnet
of Rupert Brooke's *1914.*

*There are waters blown by changing winds to laughter*
  *And lit by the rich skies all day. And after,*
*Frost, with a gesture, stays the waves that dance*
  *And wandering loveliness. He leaves a white*
*Unbroken glory, a gathered radiance,*
  *A width, a shining peace, under the night.*

This is the movement in reverse. In our more usual ways

of thought we may picture love as springtime come to earth. It is the same earth, but the sleeping bulbs are living lilies, and the trimly pruned bushes are aflame with roses. If there is no meaning in spring, then, and then only, is there no meaning in love.

But what has this to do with politics? Much in every way. Where the white man has gone in Asia and Africa, love has been so often lacking, and its absence has meant so great a loss! It is impossible to generalize on this, for there have undoubtedly been many exceptions. The settler has perhaps, on the average, been more to blame than the administrator, yet there have been many settlers from whose homes kindness has radiated. The missionary may in this field have had a better record than the administrator, but many missionaries have lacked charity. Even among some of the best missionaries there has been an unconscious arrogance — professional rather than personal. Feeling rightly that they had much to give, they have often lacked the humility to learn, and there was much to learn. A pursuit of truth together would have been a more loving attitude than the mere imparting of truth from a superior position.

This situation is not without its complications. Those missionaries who have contributed most to our knowledge of social anthropology have sometimes been lacking in missionary zeal. The combination of zeal and humility is a rare one, not only in Africa, but humility and zeal are both aspects of love.

In the same way some of the very greatest administrators have possessed that unconscious and almost innocent arrogance which today is called "paternalism." Even with it they have been great administrators and true friends, but it falls short of that love which binds men together in a really equal friendship. In the end something of great importance has been missing.

These are the almost venial and certainly understandable transgressions of the law of love. In how many cases do we find pride in a cruder form! The less the white man has to be proud about, the more arrogant, one would say from experience, are his manners. At the bottom of the social scale fear, resentment, and jealousy come in to exacerbate contacts. Whether in the United States or in the Republic of South Africa, it is the white man who has little else to fall back on who stresses the superiority of his white skin. Inferiority is the parent of bullying. Everyone in South Africa knows (if we may make another generalization to which there are exceptions) that the African is more likely to be bullied by a constable than by a judge or by a railway ticket-collector than by the Secretary for Transport.

Between the top and the bottom is to be found a kind of middle class. In British Africa men who in their own country would probably wield little authority have found themselves entrusted with vast powers over tens of thousands of people, and it has frequently gone to their heads. A kind of snobbery for which there is little real basis has done harm to the name of Britain among the Afrikaners of the Transvaal, the Brahmins of India, and the princes of Malaya alike.

In all these cases the need of love as a political virtue has been unrealized. Students of politics have quite ignored it, perhaps because they felt it had theological implications, though this, of course, is no argument at all. The facts have caught up with them. Empires, even when just, can come crashing because of the absence of love. So could a commonwealth of nations. So could a divided and unhappy world.

What love really means in political life is the recognition of the other man as a person to be cared for, to be seen in his infinite possibilities as a human being. To adapt Matthew Arnold's very inadequate definition of religion, love may be defined as justice touched with emotion. Paul Tillich calls it "Justice in ecstasy."[5] It is much more than that, but it *is* that.

5. Paul Tillich, *Love, Power, and Justice* (New York: Oxford University Press, 1954), p. 83.

It calls for an atmosphere of freedom, for love cannot thrive where there is domination on one side and fear on the other. It calls for humility, which is the simple knowledge of the truth about one's self and others. Where there is courtesy, where there is compassion, where there are such things as children's courts or adequate old age pensions paid out without humiliation, or comfortable homes for the aged, or suspended sentences for young offenders — there is love in practice. But where harsh laws attack freedom and inspire fear, where subject peoples are treated with hardness or with no recognition of their personal feelings, where laws are mechanically administered with no recognition of the human individuality of those concerned, there love is absent, justice itself is wounded, and the State cannot expect to win the love and loyalty of its subjects.

The extraordinary appreciation which Africans and Asians show for simple courtesy on the part of white men is a striking feature of any race-dominated state. Courtesy can, of course, be highly artificial: it must be more than mere manners and must go far deeper than external behavior. Where it does go deep it is greatly valued. This gratitude has elements of great pathos about it. Men are beyond measure thankful for what should be a commonplace daily experience.

Let us claim love, then, as a virtue in public as in private life. But here we come upon a great difficulty, for long experience suggests that love is not really possible except as a gift of God, that man cannot command it, that a man who does not love God with all his heart and all his mind and all his soul and all his strength cannot hope to love his neighbor as himself. We can, in some measure, do justice without realizing our need of God. We can even, so at least we feel, out of our own resources act as if we loved. But to love, really to love, is beyond us, except as a divine gift.

Thus we are thrown upon the grace of God, and what has this to do, so some will ask, with political philosophy? There have been great political thinkers, such as St. Thomas Aquinas or Jacques Maritain, who have accepted the marriage of faith and political thought with joy, but since the days of Hobbes and Locke this has become unusual and suspect. This artificial neutrality of the human mind is surely intellectually dishonest. If God does not exist, let us say so. It is a difficult thesis to maintain; but better this straightforward atheism or an honest statement that we do not know and cannot make up our minds, than the position that God does exist but that He does not matter, that He is a frill on the garment of life, pleasant indeed and ornamental but not fundamentally necessary. This, which is probably the most common academic position, is utterly untenable. If God exists He is by definition the most important fact in life.

Why do we find men, otherwise able, taking up so impossible a position? It may be a misunderstanding of the value of tolerance. Tolerance means that we give those who disagree with us a fair and respectful hearing: it does not mean that we ourselves should remain silent. Is it a fear of discourtesy or of causing embarrassment to others? Surely, though there is a right reticence in the matters nearest to our hearts, we must give our faith and love expression sometimes. Is it, perhaps, the result of the departmentalization of knowledge, so that we come to believe that theology should not intrude into politics? But man is one. He is not political man or economic man, not only an animal, not only a thinker: he is *man,* and philosophy must study the whole man. The examples of economics and psychology show us very clearly how much may be gained in clarity and knowledge by separating the facts of observation from our sense of values: they show us equally clearly how dangerous such a separation is unless we proceed to reintegrate our thinking after it.

Our need of God we may then admit. He only can keep love from being merely a set of better rules. He only can give it fresh life and spontaneity every day. He only can make it unpredictable and free. He only can make it come bubbling up naturally. He only can keep us from being conscious of it, loving ourselves for being loving, proud of our humility. In this more than anything else we are dependent on God Who is Love, union with Whom is our blessed destiny, prideful separation from Whom is the primal sin.

But, some will object, and not unreasonably, is it not putting a heavy burden on men to say that all our doings without charity are nothing worth and that God alone can give us this charity, and then to demand it as a workaday virtue in practical political life? Justice is just such a practical virtue and we may in some measure attain it, but what if we are not religious people, if we cannot warm up to that God Who alone can give us real love?

This is to assume that our receipt of the gifts of God is conscious, to throw all the stress on our outstretched hands rather than on His gift. We cannot truly love without the grace of God, but we can receive His grace without recognizing it as such. Surely we are, as far as our minds and consciences permit us, to turn to Him for sorely needed help, not to refuse in pride, for pride that cuts us off from God does make love difficult. But we may have help from Him that we do not recognize as such, and it will be like the poetic spirit in a man who claims that he can only write prose.

We must therefore not treat love as the rare attainment of saints or mystics but as something to be sought after even in the life of what we regard (perhaps mistakenly) as a secular state. It is no fugitive or cloistered virtue. As with justice, the nearer we can approximate to it the better. If right is to give law its true meaning, if love is to give right its warmth and life, if both are to limit power, then we must as far as in us lies strive for these things and recognize them as real virtues in a real state.

Through all this reasoning, life comes surging in with the

feeling that love is a most powerful thing. "Many waters cannot quench love neither can the floods drown it." Surely it is strong enough to act as that check on power which neither law nor right can fully provide.

Certainly we should give it full scope to do so. It must come naturally from the depth of men's hearts and not be a conscious political weapon if it is to do any good. Even so it may not immediately overcome evil. Joan of Arc had to face the flames before France was saved. Victory in the political sense is not entailed to love. We shall in its light have to recast the meaning of "success." What is invincible in love is not that it gets its own way but that it keeps on loving. This is the power of love in the face of man's freedom to do wrong: it is the victory of the Cross.

We, therefore, cannot bind political power fully even by love. What we can do is to unbind our own hearts and spirits. Yet even in the political field love has its victories, though we have to wait for them. The world could never be the same as if the Cross had not been. *Stat crux dum volvitur orbis.* In a lesser sphere, France could never be the same after the executioner of Rouen had thrust his torch into the faggots. Love is in the end the most powerful force in the world. Nor is any situation too desperate for it. Love can do the impossible.

By the statement that no situation is too desperate for love, we do not mean that any situation can be cleared up if only enough love is poured into it. For that very freedom without which love can have no being or value may, if it is abused, stand in love's way. Obstinate adherence to evil may defeat love or postpone indefinitely its victory in the ordinary sense of the word "victory." What we mean is that the loving person can never be put in a position where it is impossible to act. There is always something for love to do, if it is only to die.

This truth is important for we find ourselves in our own day facing situations which are impossible, problems to which we find, as the phrase goes, "no solution." The importance of the conception of love in political thought is that, deeply considered, love has always something that it can do. What it does, even if it is death, is creative.

This anyone may understand who has read the writings of Dietrich Bonhoeffer or others of the German opposition who faced under Hitler a situation which was truly impossible. Law was a mere instrument of the oppressor, justice was in chains, freedom was gone. There was no way of opposing tyranny. The only choice was between bitterness and love. The German martyrs chose love and their death was creative. It was they more than any others who enabled Germany to rise from its ashes. To the wider world they gave a vision which it can never lose.

In the days of Mau Mau the same impossibility faced the Kikuyu Christians. Some broke under it. Some compromised with evil. Some met their end with both fortitude and faith. When the true history of Africa is written after the years have given us clear vision and perspective, they will have their true place as African heroes.

Love may have to live and not to die. And here we may tell the story of Jozua Joubert. In the Anglo-Boer War of 1899-1902, Jozua Joubert lost his right arm as the result of a shot fired by a "National Scout," a Boer who was serving in the British army against his own countrymen. The end of the war came, and to Jozua Joubert all was lost. His Republic had gone. His right arm was lost. His farm was devastated. He returned to it to find that his next-door neighbor was the National Scout who had shot him. On Sunday afternoon the National Scout, sitting on his stoop, saw a man riding somewhat awkwardly up to his front door. By the time he recognized him it was too late to escape. Jozua Joubert walked up to him and held out his left hand. "Friend," he said, "we have to live together in this country and I have ridden across to shake hands with you."

In the great sufferings and humiliations of the Africans and other people of color in South Africa, this same spirit has often been known to prevail. By every canon of righteousness the man of color has much to avenge. Where love remains there is hope of doing the impossible, the manifestly impossible — building a new and kindlier society in peace and mutual respect in a divided country.

But to show that love may have a laughing as well as a tearful face, let me tell the story told to me by a Boer ex-officer more than forty years after it happened, when he was President of the South African Senate. As nearly as I can remember it, it ran thus.

In March, 1902, when peace was only two months away, his Commando captured a number of British prisoners. As they had no means of keeping them, they decided to attempt an exchange, and my friend was sent under a flag of truce to try to effect it. When he had been ridden into the British camp headquarters and the handkerchief had been removed from his eyes and he had stated his errand, it was discovered that, what with the necessity of consulting nominal lists and looking into certain other details, he would have to be kept in camp overnight.

This posed several problems to his unwilling hosts. My friend was a Veld-Kornet. The British did not quite know what a Veld-Kornet was, so they decided to dine him in the Sergeants' Mess. (They were wrong, but that is beside the point.) But this only solved part of their difficulty. Four long hours stretched out before dinner. What were they to do with him?

More in despair than in hope they asked him: "Do you play cricket?" "Oh, yes," he replied. "You, a Dutchman, play cricket!" "Yes, I play cricket," he answered again. And to further questions he answered, "Why not try me?"

Sides were picked, and my friend took four wickets and knocked up twenty-six runs. By some process of reasoning which eludes me this convinced them that the Veld-Kornet should be dined in the Officer's Mess, and dined — and wined — he was. In the mellow aftermath of a wonderful meal, he let himself talk rather too freely. "For three weeks," he said, "I have had nothing to eat but meat — literally nothing but meat. We are short of everything and now we have run out of ammunition. But somehow we are going to fight on to the bitter end."

After a good night's sleep he received his answer and his papers and was ready to return. His horse was led up to him. He noticed that his saddlebags, previously empty, were bulging; but he was too much of a gentleman to comment on the fact. He was blindfolded, ridden to the outposts, and the handkerchief taken off and the last farewells spoken. When he was over the first hill he stopped and had a look at his saddlebags. They contained biscuits, condensed milk, jam, cheese, and a quantity of .303 ammunition, together with a note explaining that they found it very unsatisfactory that so good a cricketer should have nothing to fire at them with!

I do not know if, in this particular case, love (combined with cricket) won in the long run. The recipient of the .303 cartridges remained to the end of a long life an advocate of good relations between Boer and Briton and showed a consistent example of personal kindliness. The gospel which he preached and practiced did not, it is true, succeed in commanding the support of the majority of white South Africans. But is the story over yet? Who knows what strange transmutations the history of South Africa may still undergo, and in the end incidents such as the one related may help to form the final pattern. In any case is it not a rather lovely thing that it happened?

The problem with which we have been struggling so painfully in this chapter is whether love produces political results. Our unhesitating answer is that it does. But before we conclude, it may be of value to elaborate this statement. First, "love" must not be interpreted as meaning a mawkish sentimentality or a kind of pious and placid passivity. It may mean participation in conflict, as with

> *Dante, who loved well because he hated,*
> *Hated sin that hinders us from loving.*

It may mean casting the money-changers out of our particular Temple. It may mean a searching challenge to Church and State in our particular Israel. It may mean all these things. But there are certain things that, in the nature of the case, it cannot mean. It cannot mean fear. It cannot mean hatred of persons. It cannot mean a depersonalized bureaucracy. It cannot mean treating any man as a means to an end.

Will it produce political results? This is virtually to ask whether love pays, and this is a question so incompatible with the nature of love that it ought not to be asked. Would we ask whether justice paid before we made up our minds to be just? What we may perhaps allow ourselves to ask is whether love is relevant to the political scene. Justice is, and if justice is, so is love, which is the justice of springtime. Justice is worth while for its own sake. So is love. Justice may mean a setback for the just man. So may love for the man who loves. Justice is infinitely worth while in the long run. So is love. Justice is worth doing, though the doing of it bring no visible political result. So is love. In short, we must do justly and love our neighbor both — the latter is, we insist, as relevant to politics as the former — but not to attain an already envisaged political end. On the contrary our political ends must be subordinate to justice and also to love: it is love and justice which must form the unknown end, not support some other end which we think we know.

In this discussion of the place of love in political thought, we are almost irresistibly driven to the Divine source of life, to the roots of the truly loving life. But here we must check ourselves for more reasons than one. It is not for us at this

time and in this context, if at any time or in any context, to
lay down that the acceptance of certain dogmas is essential
for the life of love. That there is an intimate connection,
there can be no doubt, and we ourselves may well have experienced that connection. But there is always the danger
that humorless, self-righteous people, smug in their own "religion," may use this argument to let themselves feel superior
to their fellow men, who may in fact know more of love than
they do. "The wind bloweth where it listeth." It may well be
that they who seek God will find Him along the road of love,
just as those who seek love may well find God meeting them
on their way to their particular Emmaus.

The place of love in politics is something which must be
arguable apart from orthodox dogma. There is in it a truth
for all, whether orthodox believers or not.

But if we are going to cut down to a minimum the reference to Christian dogma, we may be allowed to begin this part
of our discussion with a text. Christ proclaimed Himself to be
the Way, the Truth, and the Life, and it is around these three
points that we may well build the doctrine of active love in
political affairs.

It is almost impossible to exaggerate the value of the conception of the Way. For all over Africa, whether on the extreme Right or on the extreme Left, there is a tendency to fix
the end arbitrarily and to seek what would appear to be the
most efficient way of attaining that end. This is a completely
false philosophy of life, and the source of a very large number
of historical tragedies. No evil means can bring about a good
end. The goal of our struggles — let us be honest enough to
acknowledge it — is unknown. It is the Way which will determine the end. That is why we must look with the utmost
suspicion on arguments which seek to make us follow ways
that we feel instinctively to be wrong because we have a noble
end in view. It is not necessary, as we have seen earlier, to
take the view that force is always wrong. But it is necessary to

reject force merely as the quickest and most efficient means of obtaining an arbitrarily selected end, unless we are convinced that it is in very truth the best way. Liberalism can never insist enough on this fundamentally liberal doctrine and any school of politics which rejects it renders itself by that very rejection open to criticism.

In our grammar of politics, the next thing that we must look at is Truth. The Truth is a great deal more than a collection of facts, yet it begins with a collection of facts. We may today find the slogan "measurement and publicity" inadequate, but the assemblage of facts for which the old term "measurement" stands is in itself a valid and valuable contribution to political life. Too much of our argument is based on a scornful rejection of facts, or perhaps the choosing out of those facts the ones which best support our case. Truth is not that which supplies the best arguments for our political objectives. Truth has its own autonomy which has to be respected, even reverenced.

But there is more than the sum of all the facts. In this study we are being asked to revise some of our basic conceptions. We need to look at them as well as the facts which we shall in due course test by them. And the facts need to be seen through the eyes of love. Never was there a falser statement than the statement that love is blind. On the contrary it is only love which sees.

We come to the third element in our grammar of politics, namely Life. We should go out for life and therefore all that is abounding with life should be welcome in our lives. Because life is one and because we are called to go out into life, we may not neglect politics. More than one class of person may be tempted to do so. There is, of course, the unimaginative person whose whole idea of life is more or less three square meals and a bed, and who may be below politics, just as others may feel themselves to be above politics. It is the latter dangerously superior spirits whom we have mainly in mind. It may well be that someone deeply dedicated to art or to literature may feel politics an intrusion. This is not an argument to suggest that Picasso should be a member of the Chamber of Deputies, or that T. S. Eliot should run a government department. It is, however, a call to us all, most of whom, though we may be fastidious about our art, are neither Picassos nor T. S. Eliots, to see that our view of life, our very art itself, is imperfect if it is divorced from some of the most vital human movements of our time. There is also that view of religion that divorces it from politics, and there are men who make a great claim of personal religion and sacrifice much for it, but impoverish themselves and their fellow men by restricting their religion to a department of life instead of letting it become Life indeed. We might also take the question of the scientists, the value of whose work may be the same whatever government is in power. Nevertheless the scientist in becoming a scientist does not cease to be a man, and if as a man he is uninterested in the world around him, the most he can hope to be is an excellent instrument, but not the human arm that uses the instrument.

It is desirable that in whatever department of life we may be busy life should flow through us, and with life, love, which is the essence of life. Life should be full. But life should also be in one piece. We readily criticize the religious man, the artist, or the scientist who leaves politics out. But if Africans need any gospel more than another at this time, it is that the man should be challenged who treats politics as the whole of life. It is a great danger and it is particularly likely to happen in any liberation movement or in the life of any idealist who fights for liberty. Just as religion is less real and effective, less truly religion, if it leaves out politics, so is politics less truly politics, less fully what the people need, if it leaves out religion or art or poetry or science.

Some people make these mass excisions on the basis that they are narrowing themselves and their lives only for the time being until the particular end has been reached. This is an argument both dangerous and misleading. Human life and character does not stand still. You cannot set yourself a five-year plan restricted to politics only, and at the end of it find yourself the same person that you were when you made the plan. Life goes on all the time. There is no true time except the present. The diverting of any fulness of life to the future is a denial of life in the present.

If any man feels that he wants to have nothing to do with religion and does not want religion brought into this argument, let him consider science and art, let him ask himself with all honesty whether he has any right to make politics more important than science or art. All are part of life. Life is indivisible because men are indivisible. Every political movement in Africa would gain if the means were considered more than the end, if the truth were to be more than propaganda, and if love were to be more than even the warm exhilarating companionship of a great political struggle for a high end.

Were men to go out wholeheartedly together into life as a whole, every branch of life would be enriched by the strength, beauty, and inspiration of all the other branches. We would apply this thought more especially to the conditions of racially divided Southeastern Africa, whether our thoughts be on Kenya, the Federation of Rhodesia and Nyasaland, or the Republic of South Africa. It is a matter of seeking life together. What could be a greater boon to any one of these areas than a movement of the whole people into more abundant life? But this, which would bring untold blessing in its train, is resisted by many men of many different schools of thought. Afrikaner Nationalism, taking cover within its fortified laager, is afraid to go out and share in the joint life with others who are activated by the life spirit. White men of whatever racial background in Southeastern Africa are too often afraid of the sharing of life with the African. They may indeed be extremely lacking in that commodity of life themselves. Too many, alas, are. They live on the surface, and their attitude in politics is a combination of apathy, terror, and irritation.

But what of the forces of liberation themselves? Whether the soldiers of liberty be Africans or whether they be dedicated white men determined to see that justice is done to Africans, the whole tendency of the liberation struggle, influenced as it is by dubious philosophies of life from outside Africa, is to narrow life by equating it with the liberation struggle. The fight for freedom is indeed a vital part of life, but it can never be the whole of life.

Why is it that able, devoted, noble-hearted men and women striving for a right ideal should be so vulnerable on this point? Is it perhaps the result of a fear that too much interest in literature or science or religion will stand in the way of complete and selfless devotion to the liberation movement? This should not be so, but even if it were so, the question must be raised whether a liberation movement so conceived is worthy of a man's whole life. Life must be given to Life, not to a movement or a cause, but only to Life. And here a comparison with human love is helpful, for marriage is surely, at its best, to quote out of their context certain famous words of Burke, "a partnership in all virtue and in all perfection." Consider the end of a marriage that concentrated on the maximum amount of marital love. It would obviously impoverish itself at the end, even in its own sphere. Affection would cloy, passion would find itself spent, the partner who must be loved at all costs and for a lifetime would become in the end positively hateful. But true human love which is, in truth, "a partnership in all virtue and in all perfection," in art and science, religion and politics, and in every aspect of life, must encourage, enrich, and strengthen every special sphere of action. What looks like idealistic moonshine is one of the most realistic propositions of life — that when we lose ourselves we find ourselves. This is the key to the Triune wonder of Love, Politics, and Life.

*Chapter Three*

## LOVE'S LAST WORD

Love will glow more deeply if it is brought down from the heavenly places to the realities of life. These things do not degrade love: love ennobles them. The realities of political life in Africa are mainly what Africa has made of the two conceptions of democracy and nationalism, the two most potent ideals in liberated Africa. Communism, it is true, is doing its utmost to interpenetrate both, but its success is uncertain and its appeal (except as an ancillary to national liberation) limited. We shall therefore consider rather the two master passions of the new Africa. Africans have given a limited interpretation of democracy and have accorded an uncritical acceptance to nationalism. Let us examine each of these concepts in turn, and then let love have its last word on these and similar political passions.

Democracy has been defined by one of its greatest heroes as "government of the people by the people for the people." It has also been defined less rhetorically as "a state of affairs where you can change your Government without shooting it." Both of these definitions are true, yet even in combination they do not go far enough, for in a democratic state the sanctity of every human personality within it ought to be recognized and respected.

Abraham Lincoln's definition supports the case, so familiar to the mid-twentieth century, for universal suffrage. It is in this form that the claims of democracy are best understood in Africa, and it is precisely this interpretation of democracy that is repugnant to the majority of white people in Algeria or in the Republic of South Africa. It is to be noted that Britain has both accepted the principle in her African possessions, and also been most reluctant to put it into immediate effect; hence the extremely complicated history of constitutions in Southeastern Africa, with general rolls and special rolls, weighted votes, property qualifications and educational qualifications. In all this Britain has been true to her own experience of gradual extension of political rights in 1832 and the three generations which followed. African nationalist movements have been most unwilling to accept this gradualist policy, and the history of British opposition to immediate universal suffrage in the Federation of Rhodesia and Nyasaland and in Kenya has been one of a series of not very successful rearguard actions.

It seems that the case for gradualism is mainly one of expediency — the need to reconcile a previously dominant white minority to its position as a very small portion of an African state. The feelings of this minority must be understood with sympathy even if they have to be overridden. Britain, which encouraged the emigration of its own subjects to Africa and for at least half a century gave them that exceptional political position without which they would hardly have come, is placed in a humiliating position if she is compelled to force them to accept political powerlessness. Yet she is also in a false position if she deprives Africans, because they are Africans, of equal status on their own continent and in the lands of their birth, against the known wishes both of her most influential ally, the United States of America, and also of her most inveterate foe and rival for the affections of Africa, the Soviet Union. This is one of the many dilemmas challenging Britain in the 1960's.

There is a case for gradualism in the feeling that a democracy needs education and experience and that every extension of the franchise should leave the new voters smaller in number than the existing electorate. This would not, except in the very first stages of liberalization, leave the white voters in "mixed" African areas in a majority, but it would at least leave the experienced voters in a majority. There is much to be said for such a process, but it demands from emergent African nationalism more patience and self-control than can perhaps be expected from a movement fraught with deep emotion, a liberation movement. Probably the fate of gradualism depends much less on logic or political experience than on the amount of forbearance shown by tumultuous and emotional national freedom movements.

In the Republic of South Africa the refusal of the white community to give any franchise at all is met by a mounting demand on the part of the subject majority for universal franchise and nothing short of universal franchise. Few African, Indian, or Colored political leaders would undertake to accept less, even as an instalment. The more the years go by the stronger grows this feeling. It might be that, if a government able to implement its views offered a partial franchise, this would be accepted as one step in a movement to the enfranchisement of all. Similar reasonableness can hardly be expected toward the proposals of small reformist groups, unable to give effect to their views. The non-white leaders would then be giving up a great principle for ineffective support. By the time that reformers are in the saddle, it may be too late to expect such reasonableness from the impatient and voteless majority. To such a pitch has the unrealistic ideology of its government and the blindness of even its "good" people, who keep on offering too little too late, brought that unhappy republic.

Faced by such frustrating conflicts of expediency, it may be the best thing for us to consider matters of principle. Universal suffrage is hardly challenged today in homogeneous countries. Opposition to it is found mainly in complex societies and is based very clearly on nationalism or racism.

The fundamental argument for universal suffrage is the equality of man — the rights of human beings as human beings. In the moral and spiritual sense this is an invincible argument since infinity equals infinity and all souls are of equal moral worth before God and man. Nor can any attempts to argue for inequality of intellectual capacity convince us. Why should they be brought into this matter in Africa and not in Europe, unless it be a despairing effort on the part of the white minorities there to protect their privileged position by pseudo-scientific arguments? All efforts to classify the intelligence of racial groups — efforts which seem to many of us inherently unsound and unscientific — break down on that anfractuosity of human nature which invariably insists on placing the investigator's group at the head of the list. A test which placed the average of the white American group higher than that of the Negro American placed the Scots fourth only in the scale of human intelligence: could any more devastating argument be adduced?

But even if it were possible to measure the relative intelligence of races or nations, would this justify us in placing individuals of the lower group with their group and not according to their rating as persons? Moreover, what arguments can be adduced for considering intelligence as the only test of political stature? Surely character counts. Must Machiavelli necessarily be placed above Brother Juniper? And no one has yet devised a method of measuring character. If anyone ever could, it would be as misleading as racial intelligence tests have been. The white man, in his humorless moments, would place high on the list justice, honesty, providence, and perhaps courage and honor; but where would be put such qualities as love, light-heartedness, patient endurance, and worship, with which the Africans seem to be so splendidly endowed? If Brother Elias were the ideal, the white man at his best would rate high, but what if we were to be rated according to the standards of St. Francis of Assisi?

Where inequalities cannot be adequately measured, there is only one fair thing to do. It is to treat men as equals. And if men are to be treated as equals, where is the argument of principle against universal suffrage?

There is another strong argument in favor of giving all men the vote. It is that legislation affects all, and that any individual knows how legislation affects him with a poignancy not experienced in the same measure by anyone else. It is on the rock of this fact that benevolent paternalism has suffered shipwreck, and fundamentally the faults of paternalism have been unteachableness and lack of humility. Are these not still the faults of the voters who deny the unenfranchised the vote?

It would undoubtedly facilitate enfranchisement in multiracial states like the Federation of Rhodesia and Nyasaland and the Republic of South Africa if the Africans and other disfranchised groups would accept gradualism. But this, if it could be done at all, could be done only if those concerned were assured that partial enfranchisement was a step to full enfranchisement at a fairly early date. The privileged white man would thus have to face the issue of universal suffrage, and he should face it frankly and honestly now. The chief fears surrounding it are those that assume the predominance of nationalism or racism in any multiracial state, a subject that will be dealt with later. Here it may be said that nationalism, while a probability in the early stages of a newly enfranchised country, is neither certain nor necessarily permanent, and further that there is no more sure way of provoking black nationalism than the predominance of white nationalism.

Whatever course is taken, general education is, as Mill saw so clearly, an urgent necessity, whether it comes before or after the granting of the vote.

We come now to our second definition of democracy — "a state of affairs where you can change your Government with-

out shooting it." In other words, a true and mature democratic state is one where there is an Opposition which can
truly be regraded as an alternative Government. Ghana has
taken steps to minimize this possibility. Less crudely, but very
effectively, the Government of the Republic of South Africa
has done the same. Neither can be described as a democracy,
not even Ghana with its universal suffrage.

When a community has gained its freedom and emerges
as a new independent state, it is usually as the result of a
strong national liberation movement. The "moderates" or
"loyalists" are discredited by the success of their more militant
fellow-countrymen. The first Government of the new country
is almost sure to be formed from members of the liberation
movement and to possess an enormous majority. Such was
the case in Ghana. Such was the case in India. From this point
the histories of the two countries diverge. Mr. Nehru has tried
to run the Indian Parliament in such a way as to give the
congeries of small parties which oppose him the air of an
official Opposition. Dr. Nkrumah, on the other hand, has
done his best to equate opposition to his Government with
disloyalty to the state. So far as really effective opposition is
concerned, Dr. Verwoerd has tended to follow the same
course.

Perhaps it is too much to expect successful nationalist
leaders to create a two-party system, but if they wish to be
thought democrats they should at least not try to destroy it.

Is the two-party system a purely Anglo-Saxon phenomenon?
It tends, despite the emergence of a third or fourth party at
times, to remain the normal political structure of Great Britain, the United States, Canada, Australia, New Zealand, even
South Africa. On the other hand the experience of countries
like France or Israel shows that democracy can be combined
with a multiplicity of parties. But a one-party system is irreconcilable with democracy. Under it criticism becomes trea-
son, the head of the party is identified with the head of the

state, patriotism is interpreted as meaning wholehearted agreement with the Government, and freedom of speech and of the press become at best unnecessary and at worst dangerous.

If the two-party system is Anglo-Saxon in inspiration and origin, so is the cabinet system. If the first cannot be assured, should the second be part of the constitution? The Republic of South Africa is a striking illustration of the danger of introducing the forms of the British Constitution without its spirit. So is Ghana. In such cases would not the interests of democracy be better served by introducing an Executive on the Swiss model in which all shades of political thought are represented? Uruguay has in our own day found it useful to introduce a similar system.

A new state formed in the first flush of nationalist enthusiasm by a party that has almost inevitably carried nationalism to excess ought not to begin its career with a completely flexible constitution and unfettered parliamentary sovereignty. This faith in the British tradition, so flattering to Englishmen, is misplaced when the background of British tradition and modes of thought is missing. It was the gravest fault committed by General Smuts and those who followed his lead in the South African National Convention. During the last half century the history of South Africa has largely been the story of the way in which those who disbelieved in the spirit of the British Constitution have used its forms to achieve their own very different type of state. Dr. Nkrumah has done the same: it is a case of "extremes meet."

A newly formed state that has yet to build up its own democratic tradition should begin its life with a rigid constitution embodying an effective bill of rights, enforceable at law, safeguarding *inter alia* those freedoms of political association, public meeting, and the press without which a constitutional Opposition cannot exist.

Universal suffrage has been strongly defended in this

chapter. But, like patriotism, it is not enough. Like the Emperor Napoleon III, popular leaders in the new states may well say: "I wish indeed to be baptized in the font of universal suffrage, but I do not want to live with my feet in the water." It is, however, precisely what democracy demands, that a ruler *should* live with "his feet in the water." What is the object of universal suffrage but to elect a parliament? What is a parliament without an effective Opposition but an illusory make-believe, a shadow-show of real democracy?

Even where the two-party system does operate, modern parliaments need many changes to make them truly democratic. The perfecting of the caucus system and the increasing rigidity of party discipline tend to make parliamentary decisions mechanical. One of the few good things to be said of the Fourth French Republic is that in it speeches could actually sway votes and turn out Governments. Such was the position of the British Government and Parliament virtually from the days of Marlborough and Godolphin to the days of Lord John Russell. In our very different era the existence of a third party, the presence in Parliament of a few Independents, the lessening of the iron grip of the caucus, would help. So would a senate which was not a mere replica of the lower house, a feature which has been unaccountably neglected in many new African constitutions.

But even at its worst parliament is not a mere mechanism; it is not useless as an organ of democracy, provided that a real Opposition exists with some real hope of coming into office. Every experienced parliamentarian knows this. Effective Opposition speeches may not change votes — the caucus system is too strong for that — but they may and do lead individual Government supporters to question their ministers' decisions, personally, in caucus, or in the informal discussions of the lobby, or even in their own hearts. They influence the public. They may win by-elections. They may seem useless and frustrating to the Opposition member, worsted in division after division by majorities so mechanical that they can be foretold with ease; but they are not useless so long as his party has any hope of one day forming a Government.

For this an unpersecuted Opposition, a free press, and an unfettered public with a sense of political responsibility are essential. Deny these and you have no real democracy.

Universal suffrage carries with it the brightly gleaming crown of the General Will. But of what avail is this golden glory if it is put on the unsightly and ferocious head of Leviathan? The combination of universal suffrage with despotism is no new thing. At its best it produced Napoleon, at its worst Hitler, but never liberty. The people, given true freedom and education, will, through many errors, fundamentally advance the cause of truth. But the people deprived of freedom, deprived of choice, uneducated in political responsibility, may well put into office tyrants who claim to be the creatures of universal suffrage, but are in fact despots.

An uninstructed and unfree "general will" must always produce tyranny, and if not the tyranny of an "elected" despot, at least the tyranny of the majority, against which that great liberal John Stuart Mill waged such implacable war. A man need not congratulate himself on being the one-millionth part of a tyrant when he is at the same time the whole of a slave.

Almost imperceptibly we have been led from the discussion of the form and working of parliaments to the consideration of the inner and spiritual meaning of democracy.

Bertrand de Jouvenel has told us that modern students of democracy must study not only the "who" but the "what."[1] The study of the "who" is virtually over; except in a few multiracial communities the principle of universal suffrage is accepted. But a modern democracy needs to study the "what" of government no less than a medieval monarch. It too needs to have a *De regimine principum* written for it. And, as has

1. In *On Power* and *Sovereignty*.

been shown in earlier chapters, one at least of the lessons which the elected rulers of a democracy must learn is the submission of power to law. Tyranny, which is the revolt of the individual ruler against the law, is not to be justified because the tyrant has been chosen by universal suffrage. Civil liberty, which is the rule of law rather than the rule of *caudillos,* national leaders, or civil servants, must come high in the list of democratic virtues.

Equally high must come individual liberty, which must surely be defended on two grounds — first, the inherent right of the individual to make his own choices in certain matters essential to his personality; second, the advantage to the State of having citizens fully developed in freedom and maturity.

It is sometimes objected that such freedom of individual choice is foreign to African tradition, that tyranny, at any rate of a leader of his own race, is not unfair or objectionable to an African who is bred in the tradition of tyranny. This is one of those half-truths which are more dangerous than lies. It is true that Africans have a tradition of tribal solidarity, but this is not tyranny. The very few African tyrants (such as the Zulu, Shaka) were no more typical of African society than were Cromwell's major-generals of English tradition. An African chief was a close counterpart of a medieval monarch in Europe. He ruled, but he ruled under the law. What burden lay on the tribesman was the burden of all but unalterable law rather than that of a tyrant's whim. The argument from tribal tradition is much more one for the rule of law than for a "leader" chosen by universal suffrage.

Universal suffrage, moreover, was no more a part of tribal life than individual liberty. It is extraordinary that men should be found to deny individual liberty in the name of tribal tradition, who at the same time support so utterly untribal an institution as the individual vote.

As a matter of fact even under the rule of chiefs there was some individual liberty. The bounds were more narrowly drawn than Mill (or we ourselves) would approve, but there were bounds. No chief, for example, would have dreamed of interfering in the family arrangements of his subjects unless they transgressed the traditional law. On such matters the family head was himself a little king, and except where a criminal charge, such as witchcraft, was laid, his home was truly his castle.

Up to this point we have been speaking of tribesmen, but not all Africans are tribesmen. Some, including many political leaders, are largely emancipated from tribal constraints. Moreover, the new African states are not tribes. Most of them include many tribes with different customs. In all of them there is a vast field of legislation and administration where tribal law does not apply and where tribal tradition affords no guidance. These become increasingly important in the people's lives. The construction of roads, railways, and harbors, commerce in all its ramifications, public health measures, postal services, wages and trade unions, higher education and technology, the professions — all these and many more aspects of life are non-tribal and have no place in the tribal tradition.

Finally there is the impact of Christianity, which, whatever its differences of dogma or ritual, is always a force for freedom, especially the freedom of women and children, but of men also. "Whosoever loveth father or mother more than me is not worthy of me" is as true of Nigeria today as of Palestine nineteen centuries ago. Christianity has always been a powerful solvent of lesser loyalties. An African priest is no more under the uncontrolled despotism of his chief today than was Thomas à Becket under that of Henry II.

Let Africa find its own forms, but freedom is universal. Africa is different in many ways from Europe, but Africans love tyranny no more than do Europeans. Thus the case for individual liberty in Africa is a very strong one.

Although we may not push the issue of "reasonableness"

in Africa or in Europe too far, it is true that in a mature democracy men should be more and more guided by reason and less and less by mere emotion, which is a good servant to reason but a bad master. Nationalism means too often "thinking with the blood." One of the difficulties of South African politics is that the questions which really interest the voters are emotional issues. The political columns of the newspapers are full of emotional reactions and there is little of the native wisdom of British, or the bread-and-butter issues of Canadian, Australian, or New Zealand politics. When we say that a democracy needs education, we do not mean merely that all the voters should be literate, but that they should think widely and naturally, and this cannot happen when every important political decision is a matter of "thinking with the blood." An uninstructed people voting on emotional grounds for a "leader" does not constitute a democracy.

From this point of view much depends on the universities of a new country. They have many spiritual enemies to face. There is the old and bad tradition of working for results — an examination pass, a degree; of working in short for status, prestige, or a job and not for learning. This danger is found in many countries which are not new, but rarely in quite so acute a form. Circumscription to a very narrow end, the glorification of memory, the unreasonably slavish acceptance of what a *guru* or what the textbook says — these things do not make mature citizens of a democracy. I have myself read recently many essays by South African students of color on the American Civil War, in which the errors of Reconstruction in the South were exposed with a vehemence and lucidity worthy of a nineteenth-century small college in Mississippi or Alabama, without any reference to the grievances, let us say, of Indians in Natal, on which the same students would be strongly on the other side.

The other danger for African universities is an over-concentration on technology and applied science, which is natural enough in face of their countries' clamant needs. A good scientist or a good engineer would normally make a good citizen of a democracy; but there is in addition a very urgent need for a real study and appreciation of the humanities, and that reason may have its place, which is not the whole of democracy but a very important part of it.

The fact is that modern theories of democracy, especially when influenced by that most undemocratic institution the Soviet Union, are based on an exaltation of man quite beyond the experience of man in the twentieth century. This is the main argument of Lord Percy's excellent book, *The Heresy of Democracy*. Democracy is not a heresy; but democracy divorced from God, freedom, and immortality, and from every moral imperative, is certainly a heresy and a dangerous one. Actions are often justified today not because they are right but because they have the support of an uninstructed majority behind them. Man as we have seen him in the staffs of Hitler's concentration camps is most certainly not an object of worship except in a devil's Mass, and we need some fundamental standard of right, other than a majority vote, if democracy is to be worth while.

Further, as Jacques Maritain has so often reminded us, the State is only one organ of society. In the new democracies all stress is laid on the government, on the State, its leaders and its organs. The freedom of the churches and of the universities and of other private societies is, if possible, even more vital in the new democracies than in the old. Life is not all politics and man is not only a citizen. As in other spheres, so in the sphere of the State, we find ourselves best by denying ourselves, and the best democracy will consist of those citizens to whom citizenship is less important than humanity, freedom, life, and love.

We come now to nationalism, than which there are few political terms more ambiguous. The exact difference between state, nation, and race is difficult to define. And per-

haps it is even more difficult to make a correct assessment of
the factors which go to make up national feeling. Is it the use
of a common language? Certainly this is a great contributory
factor, yet French-speaking Belgians and Swiss do not account
themselves French. Is it a common racial origin? Then it is
difficult to understand American or British national sentiment. In the end we are almost driven to the point where we
say that a nation is a group of people who decide to regard
themselves as such.

But if there is ambiguity in the use of the term "nationalism," there is no doubt whatever of the reality of the political
passions that are built around that term. Nationalism is one
of the most potent factors in the modern world, and certainly
it is playing a very considerable part in present-day Africa.

And yet nationalism in Africa is in a sense artificial, particularly because it is connected with territorial boundaries
that are artificial — boundaries that were drawn up by European diplomatists in the nineteenth and early twentieth centuries, generally with more reference to the *amour propre* or
the interests of the European powers concerned than with
regard to the wishes of the Africans themselves, or even the
natural tribal and racial distinctions. A boundary line in
Africa is often a river, on both banks of which dwell men of
the same speech and tribal affiliation. It may even be, and
often is, a line of latitude or longitude. Within the boundaries thus determined are generally to be found many tribes
and many languages. Ghana is an excellent example of this,
and yet there is being gradually built up among the very di-
verse people of Ghana a common Ghanaian loyalty. Perhaps
even more striking are the boundaries of Nigeria, where differences of religion accentuate the smaller tribal divisions
and the greater ones of east, west, and north. Yet there seems
to be an arising Nigerian nationalism that is conscious of
itself, especially in reaction to the claim of Ghana to the
leadership of West Africa. It is perhaps too soon to say that

a Congolese nationalism has arisen, for in the terrible inter-
regnum through which the Congo has been passing bitter
tribal disputes have formed no small part of the difficulties
of that distressed area, but no doubt it will develop in time.

In the Republic of South Africa, the Nationalist Government has done its best to encourage what might be called
tribal nationalism. If those responsible for policy could have
their way, the Zulus would be very conscious of being Zulu
and the Xhosas of being Xhosas. This is indeed a natural
tendency reinforced by differences of language and by past
history, but almost without exception the policy of encourag-
ing this tribal nationalism has broken down before the solid
opposition of the natural leaders of the people. When an
African in the Republic claims to be a Nationalist, he is standing at least for all the Africans of the Republic of whatever
race or speech, even if he is not standing for Africans in general. If he appears as the supporter and champion of a particular tribal group he is immediately supposed to be, and often
is, a "stooge" of the Government.

It happens very rarely in modern Africa that the boundaries
of a tribal or linguistic group coincide with those of an
autonomous state. Everyone knows that even Kenya and
Uganda face real difficulties because their boundaries encom-
pass more than one tribe with many tribal jealousies. Perhaps
the nearest thing to nationalism of the European type, where
a nation and a state coincide in boundaries, is Basutoland.

When an African in the Republic of South Africa or the
Federation of Rhodesia and Nyasaland claims to be a "Nationalist," what does he mean? In the normal way he does
not stand for one particular ethnic group. Nationalism as we
know it is rather an emotion bound up with race and color.
It is, in the first place, a negative emotion, a reaction to white
imperialism, colonialism, and superiority generally. To some
extent at any rate this emotion links itself up with the tri-
umphs of Africans in other parts of Africa, and there is a bond

of color and to some extent of race that goes beyond political boundaries. It is this that makes it difficult for an honest thinker to look with complete approval on African Nationalism, and at the same time with complete disapproval on Afrikaner Nationalism, yet this combination of emotions is found in most of those people who survey the problems of the Republic from the outside. Is African Nationalism, after all, any different from racialism? It may be claimed, of course, that it is connected with liberation, that the African Nationalist is fighting for his rights to be free, while the Afrikaner Nationalist is fighting for his rights to dominate. Nevertheless there is too much likeness between the two movements to enable us easily to condemn one and praise the other. Many African national movements have combined a stout defense of the rights of the Africans with a tolerant attitude toward the white man. But it is possible for African Nationalism to become strongly anti-white, and such was the wrong turning which was taken in its early days by the Pan-African Convention movement.

African Nationalists are often accused of being Communists. Sometimes indeed they are Communists, but this is not the general position. With infinite skill the leaders of the Soviet Union have appeared before the nations of Africa as a champion of all who are fighting against "colonialism and imperialism." It is a marvelous tour de force when one considers how Communism and Soviet rule generally have been forced on the nations who make up the Soviet federation, which, indeed, is one of the greatest empires of all time, differing from British, French, and Portuguese colonial empires mainly by being situated in one great land mass, and not separated by oceans.

At a famous institution for the education of Africans it was said a few years ago that students could always be induced to listen to a Communist speaker, but if a Communist and an African Nationalist were put up at the same time, the African

Nationalist would have an audience three times the size of that which came to listen to the Communist. On the whole the connection between Communism and African Nationalism seems to be adventitious, and perhaps the honors of the diplomatic struggle rest rather with the Africans than with the Soviets. For while the Soviets are terrifying the Western powers into recognizing African independence earlier than they might otherwise have done, there does not seem to be any certainty that the African states will continue to support Communism in the new world.

We come then to the comparison which we are bound to make sooner or later if we wish to survey this subject honestly, between Afrikaner Nationalism and African Nationalism.

We tend to see Afrikaner Nationalism today as the belief of a people pledged to domination. Even today this would not be a wholly true picture, for there is much which is defensive in Afrikaner Nationalism. If we go back into history this becomes much more clear. Afrikaner Nationalism is historically the self-expression of a small people striving to be free. In the nineteenth century its relation to the dominant British Empire was very much that of the African people to the Western colonial powers in the middle of this century. The Afrikaner had to struggle at every step of his existence. He had to fight for his language; he had to fight against great odds for his political independence. He had also to fight for his right to be considered a nation at all. But for the fact that the Afrikaners are white, there is much in their earlier history to link them up with African Nationalist movements.

Nevertheless, the Afrikaners throughout the conscious history of Afrikaner Nationalism have had to fight on a double front — against the African tribes no less than against the dominating British Empire — and out of these deep emotional experiences there has arisen a color consciousness which is even stronger than anti-imperial nationalism. The Afrikaner today fears that in giving rights to Africans he is destroying the national identity, the national achievement built up through so many years of struggle, and destroying it in order to place power in the hands of those whom tradition and political experience have taught him to look upon as inferior. In the world of the nineteenth and early twentieth centuries the Afrikaner could hope that some parts of his creed would be intelligible to the civilized Western World and that he would be helped by it. Even when the British Empire and the republics were at war it was tacitly agreed by both that the black man could not be brought in as an arbiter, that white men, even at war, should stand together as white men. Today the Afrikaner discovers that he stands alone in the world. His political views have become a living anachronism. Within the borders of the Republic of South Africa he is perpetuating that very dominance of white over black that has, over the past ten years, been removed in practically every other part of Africa.

If this situation is met by a genuine liberalism which lays stress on the equal value of all men, then it is difficult for Afrikaner Nationalism to arouse any sympathy in the outside world. If Afrikaner Nationalism clashes head on with African Nationalism, then it is much more difficult to say that Afrikaner Nationalism is wholly in the wrong.

The difficulty is that in its defensive attitude Afrikaner Nationalism is adding from day to day to the strength of African Nationalist movements. Theoretically the solution, expressed in the term *apartheid,* of separate African states, might be conceived by an impartial critic to meet both sets of emotions and political requirements. But it is all theoretical. There is nothing to say that Afrikaner Nationalists wish to give to Africans anything approaching a fair share of the land of the Republic or early and complete self-government. Even at its best the policy of *apartheid* is too much one of fantastic promises of a rosy future. It does nothing to meet the legitimate aspirations of the Colored people, or of those of Indian descent. It does little even to meet the legitimate aspirations of British South Africans, once the ruling race, and now not even offered the opportunity of a tribal reserve of their own. If the policy of *apartheid* were carried out fully, justly, and at great speed it might meet some of these difficulties. Others would remain.

Suppose that an independent Zulu state, an independent Xhosa state, and an independent Sotho-Tswana state were set up, would African opinion in general be prepared to accept the little white state which would remain in a corner of Southern Africa to embody Afrikaner Nationalism in political institutions? Here we come to another of the many terms which are used loosely at the present day. Because a state is in Africa it is argued that it ought to be "African." A defensive Afrikaner Nationalism having been forced to give up so much would still have to face this point of view.

The way out has been indicated more than once previously. It is the way of faith. It is a willingness to take seriously the doctrine of the Gospel that men and nations must be willing to die in order to live, that the Afrikaner will realize more of the inherent strengths and qualities in him if he is content to serve Africa rather than to dominate it. Many will look on this as mere idealistic moonshine, but it is not easy to see that the opposite, more "realistic" point of view is getting the Republic anywhere.

Certainly one of the main difficulties of nationalism as a policy arises from the equation of the nation with the State. The *Volk* (that is, the nation) must rule the State. Surely in a state where many races and traditions mingle there is a place for nationalism which does not necessarily involve the rule of the state by one particular national group. The Afrikaner then might be right to preserve his language and many of his traditions by forming part of a larger whole and not claiming the right to dominate every other race in the country.

Here, however, we come before a major difficulty. The tradition of the Afrikaner as it has been built up across the centuries is one of color consciousness and to a large extent the maintenance of a color bar. Political nationalism has so intertwined this tradition with Afrikaner self-respect that the picture of a South Africa without a color bar would mean to many, if not most, Afrikaners abject and complete failure, the National ideal betrayed. If indeed Afrikaner Nationalism is to be bound up with the maintenance of strict barriers of race and color, those many things in it that are precious and valuable may one day crash because they cannot be separated from this evil, anachronistic thing.

There are indeed positive advantages in nationalism, particularly when any small group refuses, as the Afrikaner in his day refused, to accept the stamp of inferiority, refuses to be made merely to imitate other people, learns to appreciate and honor his own past. This is part of what African Nationalism has tried to do in its turn.

Here we come once again to the ambiguity of terms. Nationalism so understood can readily be defended, but it seems so easily to become the spearhead of a positive political program. The revolt against domination may easily become domination, whether in an Afrikaner or in an African Nationalism. Respect for the past may lead to the indiscriminate defense of old traditions and ancient abuses which have had their day and ought to be disappearing in the sunlight of the modern world. Perhaps we should apply to nationalism the words which Jacques Maritain used of "sovereignty," that it would be a good thing if the term and even the thing could be wholly banished from political thinking. We shall have seen nationalism at its best if we take it as an inevitable step between the attainment of equal human solidarity and "colonialism" which has its day of usefulness, but which can easily become an evil barrier on the path of progress.

In the light of this discussion we can now go on to listen to love's last word. It seems to be that the essence of love is self-giving. It can indeed be a reciprocal process — such is marriage at its best — but it must face rejection and still give, if it is to be love that is both pure and invincible. "He that will save his life shall lose it." "He that will lose his life shall save it." Never fully carried out by ordinary men and women, this process of losing one's life for others is at least recognized as a noble and inspiring ideal in personal ethics. We have not even begun to consider it as such in politics. No man, it is argued, can expect nations to lose themselves for others. But this is to accept a permanent division between personal and public ethics, a division which we have felt ourselves unable to accept in earlier discussions.

Nationalism has its justification and its advantages as we have just seen, but if it is unaccompanied by love it will be like sounding brass or a tinkling cymbal. The nation, if it is to claim our recognition as a real entity, must give itself. It is not exempt from the general laws of humanity.

In a sense the Roman Empire did this in its earlier days. In the fourth and fifth centuries of the Christian era Rome became lost in her Empire. Rome was not the *de facto* capital. The Emperor might be Gallic, Spanish, or Arabian. Yet somehow the Roman ideal found itself in this perhaps involuntary and only half-conscious surrender. Much more so did it find itself in the more conscious and voluntary surrender made by St. Augustine and the Christian thinkers of the West under the Gothic and Vandal invasions. Without hope of reward, men who loved Rome gave Rome up for the City of God. They were not willing to place their country first. By their sacrifice, they, in spite of themselves, preserved the Latin language and the great name of Rome for a thousand years more. In this great process Rome stooped, not to conquer but to serve: conquest was an unexpected, almost an undesired by-product. The self-giving was unconditional. There was no calculation of ultimate reward. If there had been it would not have worked.

It is not easy to find modern instances of this self-giving

before our own age. Perhaps the gift of the Ionian Islands to Greece might be quoted, though here a genuine self-giving was much mixed with sentimental philhellenism. Perhaps the peaceful acceptance of Norwegian independence by the Kings of Sweden might be quoted as a genuine if negative example. But in our own time the relinquishment of Africa by the powers of Europe and the evolution of the British Empire into the British Commonwealth contain some elements of this self-giving. True, what has been given has sometimes been given merely to avoid its being taken. True also the giving has often been tarnished by ignoble motives; by the feeling that giving may perhaps pay in the long run. Yet when all allowances have been made for human frailty, the abdication of the white man in Asia and Africa has had elements of nobility and real sacrifice about it, and the act of self-abnegation has brought with it a finding of the true self of the giving nations.

When we come to apply these same principles to the Republic of South Africa, we find that few white South Africans, and very few Afrikaners, are prepared to accept them. To save the undoubted achievement and the national identity of the Afrikaner people seems to most Afrikaners the right, and indeed the only, course. To ask for a different outlook is to ask for a higher standard than has been general among other nations in past history. Yet undoubtedly the Afrikaner people, if willing to lose themselves, would for the first time fully find themselves, would earn the respect of all humanity, would break free from restricting fears and life-destroying narrowness.

This bait cannot be held out, for goodness which aims at reward loses both the reward and itself. Self-giving must be without guarantee of ultimate survival if it is to be of real value. The motive must be purer. Since the Afrikaner people claim to be par excellence a Christian people, the appeal must be to their Christian faith. That men can center their faith on

the Cross of Christ and at the same time argue that self-preser-
vation is the first law of life would be hardly credible had it
not happened so often in human history. God is Love, and on
God's self-giving rests the only ultimate hope of humanity.
In the fact that our God has wounds rests our hope.

For these reasons we should think twice and more than
twice before we base our case for the liberation of the black
man in South Africa on prudential arguments. This is particularly futile in appeals to the Afrikaner people. Their
emotions are too deeply engaged. There is hope of winning
them by the call of love which is implicit in any Christian
faith, however twisted and distorted. Ask the highest and best
of them or of any men, and the highest and best among them
will respond. Ask mean concessions for mean motives and
even the mean will hardly be convinced. There is an inverted
hypocrisy in many of our political appeals.

Love is not without reward, but true love is rewarded in
spite of itself. Love which is worthy of the name has no limits.
It does not demand gratitude: if it does, it is to that extent not
love. The self-giving which is the essence and nature of love
knows no boundaries. To doubt this is to deny the central
experience of the Christian faith. It is also to deny the truest
and most heroic moments of our own lives.

Such a love few nations have practiced at all, and none con-
sistently. Yet it is a political virtue — shall we call it the un-
found political virtue? — and one to which we must strive to
approximate. If justice is a political virtue, so is love. Justice,
too, can never be more than an approximation in states as
we know them, but that does not mean that it must not be
tried. The world languishes because love is being tried so
little. It is imperative that it should be admitted into the field
of political thought: only so will at least an attempt at an
approximation be made.

Against the din of hatred and tendentious propaganda in
the General Assembly it is hard to feel that the United Na-

tions is committed to this course. But as in its International Court it upholds the principles of justice, so in UNESCO, in the World Health Organization and the Food and Agriculture Organization, it has begun to sponsor the idea that those who have must share with those who have not, that education, health, and food must not be the monopoly of the privileged few, but must be given to all. Here is a beginning of practical idealism, almost a hesitating and shamefaced acknowledgment of love in the international sphere. Will nationalists, old and new, will fear and suspicion, kill it after all?

For love is very vulnerable. We expose ourselves when we become its servants. As St. Augustine says, "How should our celestial city ever have come to its origin, development or perfection, unless the saints live all in sociable union? . . . But yet who is he that can recount all the miseries incident unto the societies of mortals? . . . And those inconveniences that Terence pins on the back of love, as injuries, enmities, war, and peace again, do not all these wait upon our mortality continually?"[2] But this is to be expected. When Love was incarnate, He was wounded, and in the house of His friends. The greatness of Love in that cosmic drama was that it was invincible. Love could be tortured to death but nothing could make it change its character or cease to be love. Fear and hatred were still foreign to it at its nadir. "The servant is not above his Lord," and we must also expect wounds and hope for faithfulness in love.

All this must seem to many foolishness — an intrusion of emotional sermonizing into the philosophy of politics. But has the exclusion of love been so wise? Have fear and suspicion and common sense brought us very far? Have they not given us a world where the annihilation of the human race is possible and the highest hope is "coexistence"? The wisest folly in the world is falling in love. Who would give anything

2. *De Civitate Dei,* xix. 5.

for a lover whose pulse never beat fast and who regulated his courtship by pure reason? If it is a wise folly to fall in love with a woman, fallible however attractive, is there not some wisdom in the folly of falling in love with Love? Well indeed does the Apostle say: "God hath chosen the foolish things of the world to confound the wise; and God hath chosen the weak things of the world to confound the mighty; and base things of the world, and things which are despised hath God chosen, yea and things which are not, to bring to nought things that are."[3]

We are in fact dealing here with a quality hardly tried in its fulness except by the humble and those who are thought to be a little touched in the head. Such a one was the Little Man of Assisi, who in fact was normal among the abnormal, not abnormal among the normal. Yet all of us in our private life have experienced, and even given, something of it. Can we not apply it in public life?

In all the continent of Africa the missionaries have shown this quality most. To say this is to challenge indignant contradiction. The Church is the attempt to institutionalize love, and like all attempts to institutionalize it has been sadly tarnished by human fallibility and failure. Even Brother Francis must run the risk of being succeeded by Brother Elias if his vision is not to perish with him. There have been pompous missionaries, insensitive missionaries, missionaries without the necessary humility to learn the ways of the African heart, missionaries beset with a love of power. But in general missionaries — and their wives and children — have given themselves. One in the Northern Transvaal buried his wife and *all* his children and came back to the mission field. As the African people have grown in political aspiration and in education, missionaries have been willing — often late enough, but rarely so late as administrators and politicians — to abdicate their positions of leadership and authority. They

3. I Cor. 1:27-28.

have been able to say with sincerity: "They must increase, and we must decrease." They have been reviled, and have not met attack with attack. The best have been content to serve.

The Church, because of its many and great failures, can never be wholly identified with the City of God, but it reflects, through a cracked and blurred mirror it may be, the glorious light of Love. And the State, which, because it excludes no man, carries a greater weight of evil, is yet not the City of Evil, but potentially the City of God too, and it, too, must try to reflect the light of that Love which "beareth all things, believeth all things, hopeth all things, endureth all things."[4]

In all this comes the call, difficult for man as he is to accept, to cross out the capital *I*, to have no truck with the natural egoism of man. Without this, love in the fullest sense is impossible. Happy is the man who can forget himself: if he cannot forget himself let him offer himself.[5] The *I* crossed out is the Cross, and it is true that *in hoc signo vinces*.

Come, therefore. Let us make up our minds to embark on this vast adventure into the unknown, beside which the exploration of space is child's play. The call which comes to the most prosaic of us is essentially the call of the poet, to see beauty and having seen it to follow on after it, whatever may stand in the way. Well may we join in the cry, *"Sero te amavi, o pulchritudo tam antiqua et tam nova,"* for late indeed has been our response to that ancient and yet new and perpetually young beauty. We are indeed called to that adventure in the Kingdom of Love, and once we have heard the call we are both happy and doomed men; we can never be really happy again unless we follow. What do reasonings and hesitations matter? The "towering fantasy" may reel indeed, as in Dante's great vision,

4. I Cor. 13:7.
5. William Temple, *Readings in St. John's Gospel* (London, Macmillan and Co., 1949), pp. 410-11.

*But yet the will moves onward, like a wheel*
*In even motion, by that love impelled*
*Which moves the sun in heaven and all the stars.*

We must always come back from the Mountain of Trans-figuration into the demon-haunted valley. Back, then, from these glowing thoughts, into the realities of politics. And yet even in them there burns and gleams the hope that, if enough men could love enough, the world itself might be transformed into that great world of which John Stuart Mill dreamed,[6] a world where men and nations would deal justly with one another, where freedom and order might be fully reconciled, where that portion of suffering caused by man's inhumanity to man might be swept away.

But will it be so?

Who can answer that question? It could be so if enough men loved enough. Will those men be found?

Here is one of the impenetrable mysteries of human life. Is success guaranteed if we only care enough? To questions of this kind Christ gave answers indeed, but not the kind of answers which His questioners expected. "Are there few that be saved?" "Strive to enter in at the strait gate." "Wilt Thou at this time restore again the Kingdom unto Israel?" "It is not for you to know the times or the seasons." He promised His disciples, indeed, the power of the Holy Spirit, the opportunity to witness to the uttermost parts of the earth, the grace to persevere, but He left their human curiosity unanswered. We must accept the Divine wisdom in this. We cannot know whether we shall succeed in the ordinary human sense of the term. We must surely work as if we meant to succeed but the results must be left to God: the uncertainty is the price of human freedom.

6. *Political Economy*, Book IV, chap. vi, quoted in John MacCunn, *Six Radical Thinkers* (London: E. Arnold, 1907), p. 39.

What is certain is that love will persist. I do not know if we have the right to ask more. Love cannot die if we are faithful. There will always be salt enough to prevent human society from putrefying: however deep the darkness, our little candles will not go out. Since in this whole universe of life which we inhabit love is the only thing that is fundamentally worth while, let us be on the side of love.

# Bibliography

The following books are referred to in the text or have been used in its preparation:

BROOKES, EDGAR H. *The City of God and the Politics of Crisis* (London: Oxford University Press, 1960).

COWEN, D. V. *The Foundations of Freedom* (Cape Town: Oxford University Press, 1961).

DICEY, A. V. *Law of the Constitution* (London:Macmillan & Co., 1897).

D'ENTREVES, A. P. *Natural Law* (London: Hutchinson's University Press, 1952).

JOUVENEL, BERTRAND DE. *On Power* (New York: The Viking Press, 1949).

———. *Sovereignty* (London: Cambridge University Press, 1957).

MACCUNN, JOHN. *Six Radical Thinkers* (London: E. Arnold, 1907).

MARITAIN, JACQUES. *Man and the State* (Chicago: The University of Chicago Press, 1951).

MARSHALL, HEDLEY H. *Natural Justice* (London: Sweet & Maxwell, 1959).

PERCY OF NEWCASTLE, LORD. *The Heresy of Democracy* (Chicago: Henry Regnery Co., 1955).

RIQUET, MICHEL. *The Christian Faces the Ruins* (London: Sheed & Ward, 1950).

TEMPLE, WILLIAM. *Readings in St. John's Gospel* (London: Macmillan & Co., 1949).

TILLICH, PAUL. *Love, Power, and Justice* (New York: Oxford University Press, 1954).

VERSFELD, MARTHINUS. *A Guide to The City of God* (New York: Sheed & Ward, 1958).